THE OLD TESTAMENT
AND THE CRITICS

THE OLD TESTAMENT AND THE CRITICS

TRANSLATED FROM THE FRENCH OF

J. COPPENS

Professor at the University of Louvain

BY

EDWARD A. RYAN, S. J.

AND

EDWARD W. TRIBBE, S. J.

1942

ST. ANTHONY GUILD PRESS

PATERSON, NEW JERSEY

Opus quod inscribitur: L'HISTOIRE CRITIQUE DE L'ANCIEN TESTAMENT, *auctore Iosepho Coppens, ex auctoritate Eminentissimi ac Reverendissimi Cardinalis Mechliniensis Iosephi-Ernesti van Roey et legum academicarum praescripto recognitum, quum fidei aut bonis moribus contrarium nihil continere visum fuerit, imprimi potest.*

✠ P. LADEUZE, *Rector Universitatis.*

Lovanii, die 1a Iulii, 1938.

IMPRIMI POTEST.
Jacobus P. Sweeney, S. J., *Praep. Prov. Marylandiae-Neo Eboracensis.*

NIHIL OBSTAT.
Henricus J. Zolzer, *Censor Librorum.*

IMPRIMATUR.
✠ Thomas H. McLaughlin, *Episcopus Patersonensis.*

Die 12a Septembris, 1942.

ALUMNIS COLLEGII AMERICANI LOVANIENSIS
OLIM MEIS DISCIPULIS
NUNC APOSTOLICI LABORIS ERGO
PER AMERICAM SEPTENTRIONALEM DISPERSIS
D. D. D.
AUCTOR

FOREWORD TO THE AMERICAN EDITION

The English version of my work, *L'histoire critique de l'Ancien Testament*, is really a third edition. The work first appeared as a series of articles in the review of the Jesuit Theological College of Louvain, *Nouvelle Revue Théologique*, XLV (1938). The second edition was entrusted to Casterman, Tournai-Paris. This third edition in English is completely revised and brought up to date.

In reviewing my work, I have taken note of publications which have appeared since 1938: particularly, A. Robert-A. Tricot's *Initiation biblique* (Paris, 1939); *Record and Revelation* (Oxford, 1938); and *The Haverford Symposium on Archæology and the Bible* (New Haven, 1938).

I am very grateful to my colleagues for their kindness in welcoming my work, and I thank the Reverend E. A. Ryan, S. J., and the Reverend E. W. Tribbe, S. J., of Woodstock College for having undertaken the English translation.

THE AUTHOR.

Louvain, August 30, 1939.

TRANSLATORS' NOTE: Professor Coppens further revised and augmented this English text in 1940.

FOREWORD TO THE FRENCH EDITION

Since the first World War, Old Testament historical criticism has not retained the high favor which the publications of Wellhausen and his school won for it in university circles throughout the world. Most European countries no longer enjoy the tranquillity and economic prosperity required for the intensive cultivation of literature and the historical sciences. Interest has almost everywhere shifted to the study of problems of a more vital nature and of more immediate utility, such as economics, sociology, and industrial technique. Besides, the stress of the times does not permit all the scholars who have remained faithful to historical pursuits to devote their energies to that specialized work which offers the sole guarantee of trustworthy scientific progress. Some are forced to turn to more pressing tasks, principally that of defending the fundamental beliefs and common-sense truths on which in the last analysis our Christian civilization rests.

Critical studies may have declined in importance; yet it would be incorrect to imagine that they have utterly collapsed. No matter to how great a degree work has slowed up on the Continent, especially among ecclesiastical scholars, it has made steady progress in England, has found a welcome and room for expansion in the American universities, and, despite economic and political difficulties, has always had brilliant representatives in the country which is preëminently the home of *Wissenschaft.* In a word, it would be a serious mistake to accept as a fact the breakdown of critical exegesis and to be induced thereby to discontinue work in that field. On the contrary, closer attention should be paid to the progress of a critical science no longer ostentatious and sensational but showing on that account more depth and solidity. We ought to mark its weaknesses, and, when possible, its positive advances. In other words, we must take stock of the work being done, examine its worthwhile achievements, and estimate its value. The Church, which invokes the Author of all science — *Deus scientiarum Dominus est* — is not afraid of progress. She is ready to adapt the scientific exposition of her dogmas to the ceaseless advance of knowledge. She knows that though the Deposit of Faith is eternal and immutable, its human expression is capable of further improvement. She knows too that if she held aloof from scientific connections and isolated herself in the defense of positions which are out of touch with the work of secular investigators, she would fail in her mission and run the risk of bringing into active being once more some of the causes which produced the Modernist crisis of unhappy memory.

I am convinced, then, that I shall be performing useful work in writing a survey of the copious literature published on Old Testament criticism; in noting all the movements of importance; and in winnowing the results which Catholic exegesis can retain for the clarifying and strengthening of its own scientific positions. No one would dare maintain that Biblical science can make no more progress, or that from the works published since the beginning of the century by a host of writers nothing can be drawn that is useful to us. Time has poured off the all-too-rich wine served by historical criticism in its early days. We can now judge impartially the work accomplished, note the truths which it has established, and point out to prudent exegetes the way to use it.

In carrying out my difficult task, I shall express no opinion without having scrupulously checked it, and shall endeavor to proceed only by careful analysis and thorough appraisal of all positions. My work is not intended for the public at large; but I hope that it will be of service to those who, like myself, are interested in Biblical studies and desire to advance them within the Church. If it should induce some scholars to reflect fruitfully on the problems of which it treats, I shall feel amply repaid for my efforts.

THE AUTHOR.

Louvain, 1938.

LIST OF ABBREVIATIONS

AASOR: Annual of the American Schools of Oriental Research
AfO: Archiv für Orientforschung
AJSL: American Journal of Semitic Languages and Literatures
BASOR: Bulletin of the American Schools of Oriental Research
Bi: Biblica
BWANT: Beiträge zur Wissenschaft vom Alten und Neuen Testament
BWAT: Beiträge zur Wissenschaft des Alten Testaments
BZAW: Beihefte zur Zeitschrift für die alttestamentliche Wissenschaft
ETL: Ephemerides theologicae Lovanienses
HThR: Harvard Theological Review
HUCA: Hebrew Union College Annual
JAOS: Journal of the American Oriental Society
JBL: Journal of Biblical Literature
JQR: Jewish Quarterly Review
JR: Journal of Religion
JTS: Journal of Theological Studies
NTS: Nieuwe Theologische Studiën
OLZ: Orientalische Literaturzeitung
PJ: Palästina Jahrbuch
RB: Revue biblique
Rec. Rev.: Record and Revelation (Oxford, 1938)
RHPR: Revue d'histoire et de philosophie religieuse
Th Bl: Theologische Blätter
T R: Theologische Rundschau
ZAW: Zeitschrift für die alttestamentliche Wissenschaft
ZDMG: Zeitschrift der deutschen morgenländischen Gesellschaft
ZDPV: Zeitschrift des deutschen Palästina-Vereins

CONTENTS

THE OLD TESTAMENT
AND THE CRITICS

CHAPTER ONE

BEGINNINGS

WITHIN the last few years, four new *Introductions* to the critical study of the Old Testament have appeared.[1] The first, published at Giessen in the *Theologie im Abriss* series, is the work of Professor J. Meinhold and develops what may be called the average views of the modern critical school. The second is a much more original work by J. Hempel, director of the *Zeitschrift für die alttestamentliche Wissenschaft*. The author has tried to write the history of Hebrew literature according to a new method by utilizing the resources of the still young school of form criticism (*Formgeschichte*). With these two handbooks, presenting the opinions of two distinct schools of thought, belong the work of Eissfeldt and that of Oesterley and Robinson, who seek to profit by both the old and the new methods. Such is also the policy of Stanley A. Cook. Though professing adherence to the Wellhausen doctrine, the Cambridge professor adopts with equal good will the findings of form criticism, Oriental archæology, and the comparative history of ancient Oriental religions. Now and then he even

---

1. J. Meinhold, *Einführung in das Alte Testament* (3rd ed., Giessen, 1932); J. Hempel, *Althebräische Literatur und ihr hellenistisch-jüdisches Nachleben* (Berlin-Potsdam, 1930); O. Eissfeldt, *Einleitung in das Alte Testament,* Neue Theologische Grundrisse ser. (Tübingen, 1934); W. O. E. Oesterley-Theodore H. Robinson, *An Introduction to the Books of the Old Testament* (London, 1934).

1

sacrifices this or that conclusion dear to the school of Wellhausen, but disproved by recent research.[2]

The publication of these works presents a comprehensive picture of the advance of Old Testament historical criticism in recent years. As a term of comparison in the past, we may use the singularly successful *Introduction* to the Old Testament published in 1913 by Heinrich Cornill.[3] Seven times republished, it can rightly be considered the most widely disseminated expression of the views of the Wellhausen school in the pre-war period.

The present study will first trace the early development of critical methodology and exegesis. Its second chapter will summarize the history of the reaction that set in against the exaggerations of the school. Lastly, it will attempt to evaluate the new contributions, and to propose norms for the guidance of Catholic exegesis of the Old Testament.[4]

---

2. Stanley A. Cook, *The Old Testament: A Reinterpretation* (London, 1936).

3. Carl H. Cornill, *Einleitung in die kanonischen Bücher des Alten Testaments,* Grundriss der Theologischen Wissenschaften ser. (7th ed., Tübingen, 1913). An English translation, *Introduction to the Canonical Books of the Old Testament,* was made from an earlier edition in 1906, for the Theological Translations Series (New York).

4. Among the studies used in compiling this historical summary is cited particularly A. Noordtzij, *Het Probleem van het Oude Testament* (Kampen, Holland, 1927). This work may be consulted in German translation, *Das Rätsel des Alten Testaments* (Braunschweig, 1928), by W. Kolthaus. One might also consult: L. Diestel, *Geschichte des Alten Testaments in der christlichen Kirche* (Jena, 1869); Ed. Reuss, *La Bible, Ancien Testament, 3e partie: L'Histoire sainte et la Loi,* I (Paris, 1879), 10-37; S. Berger, *La Bible au XVIe siècle: Etude sur les origines de la critique biblique* (Nancy, 1879); Maurice Vernes, *Les résultats de l'exégèse biblique* (Paris, 1890); A. Westphal, *Les sources du Pentateuque: I. Le problème littéraire, II. Le problème historique* (Paris, 1888-1892); T. K. Cheyne, *Founders of Old Testament Criticism: Biographical, Descriptive, and Critical Studies* (London, 1893); J. E. McFadyen, "The Present Position of Old Testament Criticism," in *The People and the Book,* ed. A. S. Peake (Oxford, 1925), 183-219; G. C. Berkouwer, *Het Probleem der Schriftkritiek* (Kampen, 1938); *Record and Revelation: Essays on the Old Testament by Members of the Society for Old Testa-*

I. EARLIEST CRITICAL EXEGESIS

Not until the end of the eighteenth century did critical exegesis of the Old Testament make any considerable progress. Manuals generally mention Johann Gottfried Eichhorn (1752-1827), professor of Oriental languages at the University of Jena and later of philosophy at Göttingen, as the first to secure for the critical method the right of existence in Protestant university circles.[5] Before his time, the traditional interpretation of Holy Scripture was followed in all schools, Protestant as well as Catholic. Even in those early days, however, there were a few timid attempts at critical thought, and especially noteworthy were certain trends which actually prepared the development of the new exegesis.

It will not be out of place, at the outset, to describe the traditional exegetical method against which the critical world believed it necessary to react. Dr. A. Noordtzij has written of it and the main outlines of his study are reproduced here. Starting from a narrow and rigidly theological conception of the inspiration of Holy Scripture, he says, traditional exegesis looked upon the Sacred Books much as upon documents fallen from heaven. It failed, accordingly, to take into account the part that men had played in their composition, and it virtually denied any process

---

ment Study, ed. H. W. Robinson (Oxford, 1938) ; J. Coppens, *Chronique d'Ancien Testament, 1938-1939* (Louvain, 1939) ; G. A. Barton, "The Present State of Old Testament Studies," in *The Haverford Symposium on Archæology and the Bible,* ed. Elihu Grant (New Haven, 1938), 47-78.

5. Johann Gottfried Eichhorn (1752-1827), professor at Jena in 1775 and at Göttingen in 1788, exerted a notable influence in Protestant Germany as a teacher and writer. His principal work was published in Leipzig in three volumes, *Einleitung ins Alte Testament* (1780-1783; 4th ed., 1823-1826, 5 vols.). An English translation, *Introduction to the Old Testament,* appeared in 1782.

of development in Judeo-Christian revelation. In the spirit of this entirely static conception of the religious past of humanity, sacred history was unrolled as a series of lifeless tableaus sketched by the Lord Himself, we might say, for the decoration of a church or museum. Events happen with no relation to one another and no connection with the surroundings which saw them evolve. Under such conditions, exegetes showed no interest in investigating the natural factors involved in the religious history of mankind, and possessed no conception whatever of development. What is more, they centered their attention on strictly religious incidents. They did not bother about describing the cultural milieu reflected in the Sacred Books, nor did they endeavor to reconstruct the historical setting, "the situation in life," of the happenings recorded in the Bible.

At no period in the history of exegesis, certainly, was there an absolute dearth of minds which revealed some inclination to study Sacred Scripture for their own personal satisfaction, according to a strictly objective method of interpretation.[6] Up to the nineteenth century, however, no one succeeded in forming a school or in establishing a widespread and enduring movement. The textbooks, it is true, draw attention to the meritorious efforts in Christian antiquity of the Biblical school of Antioch. Its traditions, however, did not succeed in holding their ground. The rival school of Alexandria superseded Antioch and, as a consequence, allegorical exegesis was introduced into

---

6. See Berger, *La Bible au XVIe siècle;* C. Heinrici, "Biblische Kritik," in *Prot. Realencyklopädie,* XI (1902), 119-146; P. Wendland, "Zur ältesten Geschichte der Bibel in der Kirche," in *Zeitschrift für die Neutestamentliche Wissenschaft,* I (1900), 267-290; W. Nowack, *Die Bedeutung des Hieronymus für die alttestamentliche Textkritik* (Göttingen, 1875).

the Church and entrenched itself there. The Middle Ages
show a decline in Biblical studies.[7] Only in modern times
has the historical method entered the universities and
knocked at the portal of Christian exegesis, this time to be
admitted.

Various intellectual movements facilitated this approach to the Sacred Books.

First, there was the new outlook on natural science,
particularly in the field of astronomy. In the sixteenth
century a new cosmology upset the picture of the universe
which the Bible appeared to inculcate. As a result, the
inerrancy of the Scriptures was challenged and the question of divine inspiration was raised. In the second place,
the conception of history introduced by the Humanists
found fault with a sacred history consisting exclusively of
a gallery of portraits in conventionalized attitudes. To the
enthusiastic followers of the new method, history was no
longer a matter of coldly depicting a more or less extended succession of outstanding events. It meant tracing
the living picture of a series of cultural cycles, exploring
their proximate and remote origins, and thus revealing
the mysteries of the marvelous ascent of mankind to
higher intellectual levels and greater moral perfection.
In history so conceived, there was no longer any room for
a *Deus ex machina*. In the third place, the theory of evolution put in its appearance, and soon became the shib-

---

7. It should be noted, however, that the history of Biblical exegesis
in the Middle Ages is still but little known. In the opinion of mediæv-
alists, Miss Beryl Smalley of Girton College, Cambridge, is a pioneer in
the field. See, for example, her recent article, "The School of Andrew of
St. Victor," in *Recherches de Théologie ancienne et médiévale*, XI (1939),
145-167. See also the general article of Artur Landgraf, "Die Schriftzitate
in der Scholastik um die Wende des 12. zum 13. Jahrhunderts," in
Biblica, XVIII (1937), 74-94.

boleth of positive science. Admittedly at the base of the various scientific systems of the nineteenth century, this theory worked its way into the philosophical speculations of the deists on the origin of religion.

Finally, from the eighteenth century onward, new ideas on the study and teaching of ancient literature began to spread. They were inspired in part by the celebrated controversy on the authenticity of the apocryphal letters of Phalaris, which was carried on, it may be recalled, by Sir Charles Boyle and the English philologist, Bentley (1662-1742).[8] The supporters of authenticity lost their case. The affair had very significant consequences, for historians thereafter began to raise for all writings of antiquity the preliminary question of their origin. A little later, Herder, the poet and preacher of Weimar,[9] suggested to his contemporaries that they cease isolating the study of the Sacred Books from that of the monuments of secular literature deriving from the same environment, and urged them not to deny to Scriptural exegesis the benefits which the auxiliary sciences of ancient history could afford it. "The most human way of understanding the Word of God," he wrote, "is at the same time the best and only true way." It was a bold assertion. The same idea had been broached years before — though not

---

8. Richard Bentley (Jan. 27, 1662-July 14, 1742) has been called the greatest philologist of his age. Self-taught in the elements, he went on to complete his education at Oxford and Cambridge. In 1717 he was appointed Regius Professor of Theology at Cambridge. The study on the letters of Phalaris appeared in 1699.

9. Johann Gottfried Herder (Aug. 25, 1744-Dec. 18, 1803) studied at Königsberg, where he came under the influence of Kant and Hamann. His extremely versatile mind found itself at home also in other fields, principally in Idealism and the philosophies of the *Aufklärung*. A great humanist, he successfully combined in a remarkable way "das Forschen, das Sinnen, und das Dichten."

in the same rationalistic tone — in the treatise of the
Protestant exegete J. Alphonse Turretin, *De sacræ scripturæ interpretatione tractatus bipartitus* (1728). Finally,
Niebuhr, by the publication of his Roman history,[10] introduced to the exegetes and philologists of his day a new
method of reconstructing the physiognomy of the past.
He proved that the critico-historical method could lead to
definite results surpassing in value the content of the most
venerable traditions. Niebuhr's work served as a model
for the history of Israel written by Professor Heinrich
Ewald about the same time and published in two editions
between 1843 and 1859.

The new ideas and tendencies here summarily
touched upon first took root in some liberal and Nonconformist centers. All textbooks note this by mentioning
the bold views of the deistic philosophers, Baruch Spinoza
and Thomas Hobbes. Among Protestants, the new ideas
found favor especially with Pietists and Calvinists. Thus,
the father of Pietism, Philipp Jacob Spener (1635-1705),
inveighed against the almost open adoration of the letter
of the Bible on the part of Lutheran theologians. Another
Pietist, Johann Bengel (1687-1752), was an apostle of
literal and philological exegesis. He inculcated in his
pupils and his numerous readers — for some of his books
obtained signal success — rules of Scriptural interpreta-

---

10. Barthold Georg Niebuhr (1776-1831), Protestant writer, historian, and statesman. Between 1810 and 1812 he gave a course of lectures
on Roman history at the University of Berlin. They were published in
three volumes under the title, *Römische Geschichte* (1811-1832). An
English translation, *Roman History,* by F. A. Walter appeared in 1827;
this was followed by a translation of the second German edition, begun
by Julius Hare and Connop Thirwall and completed by William Smith
and Leonhard Schmitz (last ed., 1847-1851). Through his observations
on historical method, Niebuhr exerted a deep, lasting, and beneficent influence on historiography.

tion remarkable for common sense and critical acumen. At about the same time, Calvinists, particularly in the Netherlands, were turning to a more literal interpretation of Holy Scripture. Sixtinus Amama (*Antibarbarus biblicus,* 1628) and Hugo Grotius (1583-1645) had, on occasion, made very pointed remarks on sacred hermeneutics, for example, on the historical interpretation of the prophetical oracles of the Old Law. Johannes Clericus (1657-1736) went even further than they. Among Catholics, Richard Simon (1638-1712)[11] rivaled Clericus so successfully that he has been called the Father of Biblical Criticism. Although in open disagreement on many details, these two authors shared the desire of breathing new life into literary exegesis, and in their respective Churches they met the same sort of opposition. On the other hand, independent philology, represented at the time by the distinguished scholar Johann Ernesti (called the *Cicero Germanorum*), supported the advancing wing of Christian exegetes. His thesis may be phrased as follows: Interpretation of the Bible is subject to the same laws as that of any other ancient book. While the Continent was thus debating the great problems of Scriptural exegesis, England was absorbed in tasks of erudition such as the publication of dictionaries and the careful editing of ancient texts.[12]

Ironically enough, none of these precursors of Biblical criticism originated any of those hypotheses which

---

11. R. Simon, *Histoire Critique du Vieux Testament* (Paris, 1680) ; English translation, *A Critical History of the Old Testament* (1682). On Simon and the other exegetes of the Oratory, read A. Perraud, *L'Oratoire de France au XVIIᵉ et au XIX siècle* (2nd ed., Paris, 1866).

12. The most monumental work was Walton's publication of the Polyglot Bible. Simon, *op. cit.,* 541-572 (French ed.), treats of it at length.

in the course of the nineteenth century revolutionized the history of the literature of Israel. The credit for these, if credit it is, goes to minor exegetes such as H. B. Witter, the Hildesheim clergyman whose work dates from 1711; the French physician, Jean d'Astruc (1684-1766); the German critic, Johann Christoph Döderlein (1745-1792), and the Scotch Catholic priest, Alexander Geddes (1737-1802). Witter (1711) and d'Astruc (1735) were apparently the first to discover in Genesis the presence of several source-documents (*Urkunden*).[13] The question of the authenticity of the Book of Consolation in Isaias xl-lv was first raised, it seems, by Döderlein.[14] Lastly, Geddes denied the Mosaic authorship of the Pentateuch, and to explain the composition of these books advanced the theory that the Pentateuch was made up of many independent fragments. Revised later on by J. S. Vater, a German, this hypothesis attained appreciable success.[15]

II. FROM EICHHORN TO WELLHAUSEN

To Johann Gottfried Eichhorn (1752-1827),[16] the friend of Herder and of Goethe, Cheyne gives credit for having codified the initial results of Biblical criticism and

---

13. A. Lods-P. Alphandéry, "Jean Astruc et la critique biblique au XVIIIᵉ siècle," in *Revue d'Histoire et de Philosophie religieuses* (Paris, 1925); A. Lods, "Un précurseur allemand de Jean Astruc: Henning Bernhard Witter," in *Zeitschrift für die alttestamentliche Wissenschaft*, new ser., II (Berlin, 1925), 134-5.

14. Johann Christoph Döderlein (1745-1792), professor at Altdorf and at Jena. His principal work is *Institutio theologi christiani nostris temporibus accommodata* (1780; 6th ed., 1797). See W. Caspari, *Lieder und Gottessprüche der Rückwanderer (Jesaja 40-55)*, Beihefte zur Zeitschrift für die alttestamentliche Wissenschaft, 65 (Giessen, 1934), 203 ff.

15. On Alexander Geddes, read Cheyne, *op. cit.*, 1-12.

16. On J. G. Eichhorn, read Cheyne, 13-26.

determined the principles of "historico-critical" *Introductions* to the Old Testament (1780-1783). We find the term itself, apparently for the first time, in the title of the book published in 1794 by Georg Lorenz Bauer. A critic pointed out the value of Eichhorn's work when he said that Eichhorn had made nineteenth-century Germany read Baruch and therefore had contributed most, after Luther, toward incorporating into the religious literature of Germany the beauties, style, metaphors, and typical expressions of the Bible. Whatever may be thought of this general literary influence, Eichhorn's *Introduction* did succeed in bringing liberal Protestants to admit the comparatively late origin of Deutero-Isaias (xl-lvi), the Book of Daniel, Ecclesiastes, and the Book of Esther. The name of Eichhorn, however, is especially linked with the views which he developed on the composite character of the books of Moses and the hypothesis which he proposed in explanation. He suspected in Genesis the presence of two documents, later called the Priestly Code and the Book of the Yahwist, and he advanced the hypothesis of documents so successfully that the composition of the Pentateuch became the crucial problem of nineteenth-century exegetical discussion.

Propagated in the university circles of Germany by Johann Eichhorn, the hypothesis of documents was soon supplemented on an important point by Karl David Ilgen (1763-1834), his successor at Jena. This scholar seems to have been the first to sense the presence of a second Elohistic document which subsequent critics have designated simply the Elohist.[17]

---

17. On K. D. Ilgen, read Cheyne, 26-30. Ilgen, *Die Urkunden des ersten Buches von Moses in ihrer Urgestalt* (Halle, 1798).

Scarcely had the documentary theory been launched when it threatened to run aground on the sandbars of rival critical hypotheses, namely, the hypothesis of fragments, mentioned above, and the hypothesis of complements or interpolations. The latter attracted very wide attention because of the support it received from Martin Leberecht de Wette (1780-1843), an exegete who, for many reasons, but chiefly for his researches on the composition of Deuteronomy, should be ranked among the founders of the critical school. As a matter of fact, it was de Wette who brought Deuteronomy into prominence (1802-1805), thus aligning himself with J. S. Vater. He it was who assigned it to the reform of King Josias and who invented the theory of a *pia fraus* to explain the attribution of the code to the great lawgiver of the Hebrews. It may be recalled here that as early as 1828, Gramberg made an unsuccessful attempt to refloat the Eichhorn-Ilgen documentary theory, and also tried, again without success, to make Deuteronomy a product of post-Exilic Judaism. The work of salvaging the hypothesis of documents was not accomplished until 1853, by Hermann Hupfeld (1796-1866), exactly one hundred years after the publication of the dissertations of d'Astruc.[18]

In the meantime, an exegete who figures in the history of Biblical interpretation as an outsider in the grand manner displayed a literary activity as prolific as it was heterogeneous. This was Heinrich Georg August Ewald

---

18. On M. L. de Wette, read Cheyne, 31-54; C. P. Gramberg, *Libri Geneseos secundum fontes rite dignoscendos adumbratio* (Leipzig, 1828); H. Hupfeld, *Die Quellen der Genesis und die Art ihrer Zusammensetzung* (Berlin, 1853).

(1803-1875), professor at Tübingen and Göttingen.[19] Endowed with a penetrating mind and indefatigable energy, Ewald had begun his career with a well-written though violent tract against the *Beiträge* of Leberecht de Wette. In this diatribe he defended the Mosaic origin of the Pentateuch. Twenty years old at the time, Ewald, his biographers tell us, later regretted this publication as a piece of youthful folly. In 1831 he was converted to a theory which can safely be considered documentary. He distinguished two sources, the First Elohist and the Yahwist, and beside them he placed the work of an anonymous *Ergänzer* who fused and developed them. Indeed, since he accepted the theory of Leberecht de Wette (1805) in regard to Deuteronomy, Ewald can be said to have divided the Pentateuch into four documents, the Priestly Code, the Yahwist, the *Ergänzer,* and Deuteronomy. Thus he finally propounded a new form of the documentary theory. Let us observe however that, at the time, Deuteronomy was studied as a document whose origin had nothing in common with that of the

---

19. On H. Ewald, read Cheyne, 66-118. It is certainly not easy to summarize Ewald's shifting lines of reasoning. In his book, *Composition der Genesis* (1823), he vindicates exclusive Mosaic authorship. In 1831, influenced by Gramberg's *Libri Geneseos secundum fontes rite dignoscendos adumbratio,* he proposes a documentary theory in an article in *Theol. Studien und Kritiken.* The importance here attached to the First Elohist (P) contributed largely to paving the way for the success of the hypothesis of complements adopted by de Wette, von Bohlen, Tuck, Bleek, Stähelin, and Bertheau. This theory of complements was equally favored by Gramberg's and Stähelin's critical study of the Yahwist. See Westphal, *Les Sources du Pentateuque,* I (Paris, 1888), 185-6, 189-190. For Ewald's final positions, see among others, Reuss, *La Bible: I. L'Histoire sainte et la Loi* (Paris, 1879), 25. Reuss classes with Ewald two other outsiders of more modest endowments, A. Knobel (*Commentar über den Pentateuch und das Buch Josua,* 1852-1861), and M. Nicolas (*Etudes critiques sur la Bible,* 1862). The hypothesis of fragments adopted but not sustained by Ewald finally collapsed before the all-too-evident literary unity of the sections attributed to the First Elohist, the future Priestly Code.

other Mosaic books, which were sometimes grouped under the strange name of *Protonomium*. One of the characteristics of the documentary hypothesis in its final form was that it absorbed the authors or compilers of Deuteronomy into the constitutive process of the Hexateuch. Ewald's article contributed much to the acceptance of the First Elohist (P) as the *Grundschrift* or fundamental part of the Pentateuch. The reasons advanced for this were: that it was the most ancient document, and that it was the one which served as the framework wherein later additions found place.

Ewald however did not adhere to his own conclusions. At the end of his career he "burned what he had adored" and made himself a champion of the hypothesis of complements. "It is said that the aloe blooms but once," remarked Westphal, "namely, when it feels death stealing over it. The hypothesis of complements imitated the aloe: it blossomed in the last great critical work of Ewald, and then died." The great exegete relied on an extremely complicated theory of fragments and complements when he undertook to write his history of Israel (1843-1855). The originality of this work in its day has been pointed out elsewhere.

The singular views of Ewald did not, of course, find much favor with his contemporaries; instead, they augmented the prevailing confusion. The consequent uncertainty and disorder paved the way for the eventual rehabilitation of the documentary theory, which could not, at least, be charged with having lacked plausibility or clarity.

The revival of this theory was the work of Hupfeld and also to a certain extent of Riehm. In 1853, Hupfeld published a book entitled *Die Quellen der Genesis und die Art ihrer Zusammensetzung.* It was a new and eloquent plea for the hypothesis of documents as applied to Genesis.[20] The work met with such acclaim that it may be considered as furnishing the basis of the second documentary theory, which succeeded all the more quickly in winning adherents because the offensive was supported, as far as Deuteronomy was concerned, by Riehm. In 1854 he issued a monograph which revived the theory of Martin Leberecht de Wette and presented it so convincingly that it has found favor with the greater number of independent exegetes ever since. Although a few authors here and there, Knobel for example, still clung to the tenets of Ewald, the majority of critics finally rallied to the conclusions of Hupfeld and Riehm. Mention may be made of Edward Boehmer, Franz Delitzsch "the venerable," August Dillmann, one of the greatest advocates of Christian Orientalism, and especially Eberhard Schrader and Theodor Nöldeke.[21]

---

20. On H. Hupfeld, read Cheyne, 149-155. Hupfeld, *Die Quellen der Genesis.*

21. On Franz Delitzsch, read Cheyne, 155-171. Franz Delitzsch (1813-1890) taught exegesis at Rostock (1846-1850), Erlangen (1850-1867), and Leipzig (1867). He published numerous works on the Old Testament and on Judaism in the New Testament. His translation of the New Testament into Hebrew was considered a masterpiece. There are various editions of it, notably one for use in Christian preaching to the Jews, *Siphre Hab-berith Ha-Chadashah* (new ed., London, British and Foreign Bible Society, 1923). In the past century, Delitzsch represented the conservative wing of Protestant exegesis while Dillmann symbolized the moderate critical school. August Dillmann (Illingen, 1823-1894) taught at the Universities of Tübingen, Kiel, Giessen, and Berlin. His professorship in the capital of the Reich brought him to the peak of honor if not of influence. The numerous editions of his commentary on the Hexateuch in the *Kurzgefasstes Exegetisches Handbuch* series (Knobel wrote for it before him) enabled him frequently to express his critical views on the origin of the Mosaic books. Space forbids dwelling on the eccentric, complex personality of Paul de Lagarde (pseudonym of Paul Anton Bötticher, 1827-1891). Friedrich Rückert inspired him with

The hypothesis of documents, however, had to undergo another transformation before attaining to its present-day form. This was the complete reversal of the chronological order of the documents. From a perusal of his work, it appears that Hupfeld, like his predecessors, unhesitatingly ranked the First Elohist (P), or the Priestly Code, as the most ancient document. But this arrangement, common since the days of Eichhorn, was to be abandoned completely. No doubt the Priestly Code will continue to be considered in a certain sense the *Grundschrift* or basic document. Many authors will continue to hold that it served as the basis for the final fusion of the four documents, while adhering to the opinion that, of the four sources, the First Elohist (P) is the most recent, dating from the Exile and indeed, in great part, from the period of the Second Temple.

This important modification, the distinguishing characteristic of the third documentary theory, was due in part to the influence exerted on the interpretation of the First Elohist by the ideas of de Wette, George, and Vatke anent the development of religious institutions among the Israelites. The critical school agreed with these authors in considering the content of the Priestly Code to be a reflection of comparatively late Israelite theology and in attributing its composition to the time of the Babylonian Captivity and the post-Exilic restoration. Edouard Reuss

---

a love for the Oriental; from Karl Lachmann he inherited his enthusiasm for textual criticism and its methods; and from Jakob Grimm he imbibed the romantic patriotism that made him a pronounced anti-Semite and a forerunner of the Nazi movement. He did not cultivate connections and consequently was forced to publish his works at his own expense. He succeeded Ewald at Göttingen — and a strange succession it was! While there, he devoted himself chiefly to critical studies on the Septuagint. In his few pages on the question of the Pentateuch he does not hesitate to lend the weight of his authority to the solution of the critics.

(1833) and his pupil Karl Heinrich Graf (1866) were the first to hold *ex professo* for the post-Exilic origin of the Priestly Code, though only in its legislative sections.[22] In 1868 Kosters adopted these conclusions and extended them to the historical elements of the Code — a procedure which Graf was quick to second.[23] In 1869-1870, Abraham Kuenen, at that time perhaps the most esteemed of critics, announced his conviction that Graf's new chronology of the documents was correct.[24] Kuenen's adherence to the movement was interpreted as a genuine critical conversion, and the exegete himself thought it proper openly to emphasize the full significance of the step he had taken. In 1874 the controversy was decided in favor of Graf's chronology. After a reëxamination of the narrative sec-

---

22. Edouard Reuss (1804-1891), professor at Strassburg, published in several volumes a translation of the Old Testament, to which he added a copious commentary, *La Bible: Traduction nouvelle avec introduction et commentaire* (Paris, 1874). See this work, I, 32-36, and 23, note 1. — Karl Heinrich Graf (1815-1869) was a pupil and friend of Reuss. He was never a member of the University faculty, and owes his reputation to his work of 1866, *Die geschichtliche Bücher des Alten Testaments.* See A. Causse, "La Bible de Reuss et la Renaissance des études d'histoire religieuse en France," in *RHPR,* IX (1929), 1-31; also printed separately (Paris, Alcan, 1929).

23. Willem Hendrik Kosters (Enschede, 1843-1897) succeeded Kuenen at the University of Leyden and remained there until his death. In his early career Canon Albin Van Hoonacker engaged him in controversy on the history of the Jewish restoration after the Babylonian exile. See Coppens, *Le chanoine Albin Van Hoonacker: Son enseignement, son oeuvre et sa méthode exégétiques* (Paris, Desclée De Brouwer, 1935), 39-53. Kosters' work is entitled, *De Historiebeschouwing van den Deuteronomist met de berichten in Genesis-Numeri vergeleken* (Leyden, 1868). The author cites among his precursors P. von Bohlen, W. Vatke, and J. F. L. George.

24. Abraham Kuenen (Haarlem, 1828-Leyden, 1891), leader of the Dutch critical school. Scarcely twenty-four years of age when he was appointed professor at Leyden, he worked with Scholten and Opzoomer in bringing about what may be called Protestant Modernism. So great was his prestige that in the opinion of Kamphausen, Kuenen's work alone would justify foreigners in studying the language of Holland. Karl Budde, one of his many pupils, did much to spread his ideas in Germany, especially by publishing some of his studies in German, under the title, *Gesammelte Abhandlungen* (1894).

tions of the Priestly Code, Kayser confirmed the views of Graf in full. "Since the compilation and publication of the books of Chronicles," he concluded, "the true picture of the history of Israel has been completely reversed. A false perspective had formerly been obtained by the arbitrary projection of the Priestly Code into the very beginnings of the people of Israel."[25]

Kayser's monograph appeared just before Julius Wellhausen entered the controversy on the origin of the Pentateuch. The problem, as will be readily admitted, had virtually been solved before the intervention of the man who has given his name to the third documentary theory. At first sight, the fact is surprising. Its explanation lies in Wellhausen's success in giving this theory its classic expression. His exposition is remarkable, if not always for perspicuity and directness, at least for reasoning power and conviction. Furthermore, he applied the critical theory to the details of the various books forming the Hexateuch. His first articles attracted much attention, since at the very moment criticism was preparing itself for the attack and Bernhard Duhm's study of the prophets, *Die Theologie der Propheten* (1875), had sounded the clarion call for another general onslaught against the positions of traditional exegesis.[26]

---

25. August Kayser (1821-1885), a pupil of Reuss, was like his master a professor at Strassburg. He wrote *Das Vorexilische Buch der Urgeschichte Israels und seine Erweiterungen: Ein Beitrag zur Pentateuchkritik* (Strassburg, 1874).

26. Bernhard Duhm, *Die Theologie der Propheten als Grundlage für die innere Entwicklungsgeschichte der israelitischen Religion dargestellt* (Bonn, 1875). Duhm (Bingum, East Friesland, 1847-Aug. 31, 1928) taught exegesis at Göttingen and Basel (1888-1928). He was closely associated with Julius Wellhausen and justly deserves to be considered the co-founder of the Wellhausen school of criticism. From the beginning of his career, prophetic literature was his chosen field. His commentary on Isaias marked the high point of his activity.

III. Wellhausen and His School

Wellhausen's output was considerable and he maintained his viewpoint with extraordinary consistency. The conclusions of his early researches, published in a series of articles under the title, *Die Composition des Hexateuchs* (1876-1877), and in book form in 1885, 1889, and 1899, indicated the general outlines of the system whose success he was to assure.[27] The English exegete Arthur S. Peake did not exaggerate when he wrote that the year 1876 was as important in the history of Old Testament criticism as 1870, when Kuenen embraced the opinion of Reuss and Graf on the date of composition of the Priestly Code.

Though the articles which Wellhausen published in 1876 struck a telling blow, his doctrine only made its triumphal entry into learned circles two years later with the appearance of his *Geschichte Israels,* a work later reprinted under the title, *Prolegomena zur Geschichte Israels* (1883). Conscious of having broken with the traditional positions of Protestantism and specifically with those of the theological faculty at Greifswald, Wellhausen in 1882 resigned his chair at the university, "freely and in

---

27. J. Wellhausen (Hameln, 1844-Göttingen, Jan. 7, 1918), professor at Greifswald (1872-1882), Halle, Marburg, and Göttingen (1892-1913). While at Greifswald, he quit the Protestant theological faculty and joined that of philosophy and literature. His most influential works were: *Die Composition des Hexateuchs* (3rd ed., 1899); *Reste arabischen Heidentums* (2nd ed., 1927); *Israelitische und Jüdische Geschichte* (8th ed., 1921); *Prolegomena zur Geschichte Israels* (6th ed., 1927). The last two works have been translated into English: *Sketch of the History of Israel and Judah* (1891); *Prolegomena to the History of Israel,* with preface by W. Robertson Smith (3rd ed., 1886). Wellhausen became known and appreciated in English-speaking circles through his synthesis, "Israel," in the 9th edition of the *Encyclopædia Britannica* (1879). The importance of this famous edition is recognized by J. L. Garvin in the preface to the 14th edition, I (1929), xi-xii.

the conviction that he could no longer adhere to the Evangelical Church or even to Protestantism" ("Freiwillig in
dem Bewusstsein durchaus nicht mehr auf dem Boden
der evangelischen Kirche oder des Protestantismus zu
stehen").

The critical program formulated by Wellhausen provoked the most vehement protests from conservative
exegetes and particularly from those referred to in the
polemics of the day as "the saving sextet" ("das rettende
Sechsgespann"). Nevertheless Wellhausen carried the
day in German university circles. The brilliance of his
writings — their engaging and convincing tone, fine exposition of the problems, clever and orderly presentation of
arguments — assured that. Cornill declared as early as
1892: "Wellhausen should attribute his striking success
to the relative simplicity of his system and to its perfect
coherence" ("Einfachkeit und Geschlossenheit"). It was
often said of his theory that it bore the unadorned stamp
of truth, *simplex veri sigillum*. It may be added that
Wellhausen very skilfully and successfully set up his
critico-literary conclusions in the framework of a new
history of the Jewish religion, and indeed insinuated
them into a comprehensive history of religion in the ancient East. It is well known, of course, that he used the
popular traditions of pre-Islamic Arabia as a guide in his
interpretation.

From 1878 onward, Wellhausen's critical principles
steadily conquered one country after another. In Germany
the universities offered scarcely any resistance to the infil-
tration of the new ideas. The Graf-Wellhausen theory
was set forth in the *Introductions* of Carl Steuernagel and
Heinrich Cornill, and, in the matter of literary criticism

of the Hexateuch at least, even in the *Introduction* of Eduard König, the spokesman of conservative Protestant exegesis.[28] It colored the history of the religious beliefs of the Israelites as outlined in the handbooks of Schultz, Smend, Stade, Kautzsch, and Bertholet.[29] Finally, it inspired the two leading Protestant commentaries of the age, the *Handkommentar* of Wilhelm Nowack and, to an even greater extent, the *Kurzer Handkommentar* of Karl Marti.

Biblical science even now is comparatively young in the United States, but the influence of imported German professors was considerable here. The critical movement was soon under way. Charles A. Briggs, the founder of American scientific exegesis, and a collaborator and rival of the Englishman Samuel Driver, was a pioneer.[30] The field of critical research was widened by Henry Preserved Smith of the Union Theological Seminary, Paul Haupt of Johns Hopkins University, editor of the famous "Rainbow

28. C. Steuernagel, *Lehrbuch der Einleitung in das Alte Testament mit einem Anhang über die Apokryphen und Pseudepigraphen* (*Tübingen,* 1912); Cornill, *Einleitung in die kanonischen Bücher;* E. König, *Einleitung in das Alte Testament mit Einschluss der Apokryphen und der Pseudepigraphen des Alten Testaments* (Bonn, 1893).

29. H. Schultz, *Alttestamentliche Theologie: Die Offenbarungsreligion auf ihrer vorchristlichen Entwicklungsstufe dargestellt* (Göttingen, 1889); in English translation, *Old Testament Theology* (1892); R. Smend, *Lehrbuch der alttestamentlichen Religionsgeschichte* (Freiburg in Breisgau-Leipzig, 1892; 2nd ed., 1899); B. Stade-A. Bertholet, *Biblische Theologie des Alten Testaments* (Tübingen, 1905-1911), 2 volumes; E. Kautzsch, *Biblische Theologie des Alten Testaments* (Tübingen, 1911); Bertholet, *Kulturgeschichte Israels* (Göttingen, 1919), in English translation, *A History of Hebrew Civilization* (London, 1926), by A. K. Dallas.

30. Charles A. Briggs (New York, 1841-1913) taught exegesis at the Union Theological Seminary from 1874 until the year of his death. In 1892 he was excluded from the Presbyterian Church and joined the Protestant Episcopalian. See Cheyne, 229.

Bible,"[31] and William Rainey Harper, the distinguished organizer of Oriental studies in Chicago. Other scholars who did good work of a less striking nature include George Foote Moore and Crawford Howell Toy of Harvard, and Charles Cutler Torrey of Yale. Finally, the school of Wellhausen recruited a certain number of adherents from liberal Judaism. Of these Julian Morgenstern is one of the best qualified representatives.[32]

By a curious interplay of circumstances, the beginnings of critical exegesis in England trace back to three men belonging to quite different milieus: Alexander Geddes (1737-1802), a Catholic priest of Scotch origin, Bishop John William Colenso (1814-1883), of the Anglican Church, and Samuel Davidson (1806-1899), an Irish Congregationalist.[33] Thus the soil was more or less prepared for Wellhausenism.

The system made rapid progress, at least as far as its literary conclusions were concerned, as a result of the efforts of three men: W. Robertson Smith of Cambridge, Thomas Kelly Cheyne, professor at Oriel College, Oxford, and Samuel R. Driver, canon of Christ Church and profes-

---

31. On Paul Haupt and the *Regenbogenbibel* (also called the Polychrome Bible), read L. Hennequin, "Haupt (Paul)," in *Dictionnaire de la Bible: Supplément*, III (1938), col. 1408-9. — Paul Haupt (Görlitz in Silesia, Nov. 25, 1858-Baltimore, Dec. 15, 1926) taught Semitic languages at Johns Hopkins University over a period of more than forty years, up to the eve of his death.

32. G. F. Moore (1851-May 16, 1931), professor at Harvard University; C. H. Toy (1836-May 12, 1919), professor at Southern Baptist Theological Seminary and later at Harvard; Charles C. Torrey (East Hardwick, Vermont, b. Dec. 20, 1863), professor of Semitic languages at Yale since 1900; J. Morgenstern (St. Francisville, Illinois, b. March 18, 1881) studied in Berlin and Heidelberg; professor at Hebrew Union College since 1907. Consult *Who's Who in America,* XVIII (Chicago, Marquis Co., 1934).

33. See Cheyne, 4-11, 196-204, 208-210.

sor of Oxford.[34] These leaders showed rather divergent characteristics. Robertson Smith has been lauded for his creative imagination, Thomas Cheyne for his youthful impetuosity, and Samuel Driver for his erudition and prudent balance. The middle course favored by Anglican exegesis in their day may be conceived as the resultant of these opposing tendencies. The prestige of Cheyne had vanished before he reached the end of his career because he squandered his brilliant talents on arbitrary corrections of the Masoretic text and on fantastic critico-literary hypotheses. With Samuel Driver the case was quite different. As he advanced in years, he took on more and more the appearance of a high-priest. His moderate critical *Introduction* to the books of the Old Testament, his dictionary of Biblical Hebrew, and his excellent monograph on the relation of ancient Oriental archæology to Biblical history, won him exceptional prestige, the more so as he remained aloof from the religious liberalism of Wellhausen. The best English exegetes of our time are connected with the spiritual school of Driver. They include: George Buchanan Gray (d. 1922), Charles Fox Burney (d. 1925), John Skinner (d. 1925), and Arthur Samuel Peake (d. 1929). It may be mentioned in conclusion that at the very time when the literary theory of Wellhausen had completed its conquest of the universities, J. Estlin Carpenter and Canon G. Harford Battersby published an

---

34. Samuel Driver (Southampton, 1846-Feb. 28, 1914) ; see Cheyne, 248-372. W. Robertson Smith (1846-1894) began as professor at Free Church College, Aberdeen; attracted to the theories of Kuenen and Wellhausen, he published in the *Encyclopædia Britannica* various articles on the Bible which cost him his professorship in 1881. In 1883 he was appointed Lord Almoner's Professor of Arabic at Cambridge. See Cheyne, 212-225. Thomas Kelly Cheyne (London, 1841-1915), professor at Oriel College, Oxford; canon of Rochester.

important synthesis, *The Oxford Hexateuch*. Here the critico-literary problem is set forth fully down to the last detail.[35]

All things considered, the penetration of Wellhausen's ideas into England can scarcely be called an invasion. It had nothing about it which resembled a storm sweeping away previously accepted opinions. Driver maintained too close a watch over the importation of German hypotheses to allow that to happen. In the Netherlands, on the contrary, the university centers were literally flooded by the advancing tide of critical ideas. Abraham Kuenen, the reader will recall, adopted the Graf-Wellhausen theory in a manner which created a sensation. After him came a succession of scholars all of whom followed the same line as their master — Valeton, Kosters, Wildeboer, Pierson, Oort, Hooykaas.[36] The writers of this school left two monuments of their activity: the great history of Israel by Abraham Kuenen and the Dutch Bible of Leyden, *Het Oude Testament opnieuw uit den grondtekst overgezet,* published in 1899-1901 by H. Oort. In addition, Pierson issued a popular treatment of the school's conclusions in the *Geestelijke voorouders* series, under the title: *Israël* (Haarlem, 1904; 2nd edition, 1913).

---

35. J. E. Carpenter-G. Harford Battersby, *The Composition of the Hexateuch* (London, 1902). — For a selective bibliography of publications on Sacred Scripture in English, see *A Scripture Bibliography for the Use of Teachers in Secondary Schools and Bible Students* (2nd ed., London, n.d. [1937]).

36. J. Valeton (1849-1912), W. H. Kosters (1843-1897), G. Wildeboer (1855-1912), A. Pierson (1831-1896), H. Oort (1836-1927), I. Hooykaas (1837-1893). Of this group, Wildeboer represents the middle position; Oort was one of the last survivors of the modern school. See F. M. T. Böhl, *Het Oude Testament, Bijbelsch-Kerkelijk Woordenboek,* I (Groningen, 1919).

In French-speaking countries, the general spread of Wellhausenism was much less rapid. However, liberal Protestantism in France and Switzerland adopted its critico-literary conclusions very readily since it counted among its adherents the eminent Biblical scholar Edouard Reuss (1804-1891), who was one of Graf's precursors. Among other followers of the critical school we may mention Charles Bruston, professor at Montauban, Charles Piepenbring of Strassburg, Lucien Gautier of Lausanne, Alexandre Westphal of Paris, and with reservations, two decidedly individualistic writers: Antonin Causse of the University of Strassburg and Adolphe Lods of the Sorbonne. Gautier published the best *Introduction* to the books of the Old Testament that has appeared in French.[37]

Besides the group of Protestant writers, a few rationalistic exegetes likewise lent their support to the spread of these critical ideas in France. The position of Ernest Renan, who had been deeply influenced by Ewald, lacked definiteness; while that of Alfred Loisy, though not devoid of a certain flashy brilliance, betrayed the radicalism which eventually brought discredit on the Wellhausen system.[38]

---

37. L. Gautier, *Introduction à l'Ancien Testament* (2nd ed., Lausanne, 1914). Reuss, *La Bible: Traduction nouvelle.* — Westphal *Les Prophètes: Leurs écrits, leur doctrine, leur action dans les pages de la Bible hébraïque* (Paris, 1924), 2 vols. — Lods, *Israël: Des origines au milieu du VIIIᵉ siècle* (Paris, 1930); trans., *Israel from its Beginnings to the Middle of the Eighth Century,* by S. H. Hooke (New York, Knopf, 1932).

38. E. Renan, *Histoire du Peuple d'Israël* (Paris, n.d. [1887 —]), 5 vols.; trans., *History of the People of Israel,* by J. H. Allen and Mrs. E. W. Latimer (1888-1896). Critics think that this work when compared with his *Histoire des Origines du Christianisme* shows Renan to be already in decline. — A. Loisy, *La religion d'Israël* (2nd ed., revised and augmented, Ceffonds, 1908; 3rd ed., revised and augmented, Paris, 1933). A first edition of 300 copies appeared in 1901, but it was never put on sale; now rare, it is an important publication. In it Loisy "attempted to

IV. Classical Wellhausenism

A pause may be made here in this historical exposition to present briefly and schematically the principles according to which the liberal wing of the Wellhausen school commonly interpreted the literature of ancient Israel and the religious history of the Chosen People.

A. *Presuppositions:*

The Wellhausen hypothesis, at least when it includes religious liberalism, rests on three easily discernible postulates. First, its supporters profess an almost absolute skepticism toward documents relating the history of ancient Israel. Second, they accept the fundamental thesis of evolution as applied to the general trend of religious and cultural history of ancient peoples, the Hebrews included. Finally, they postulate the law of immanence in order to explain this history and consequently they reject, *a priori,* any appeal to supernatural intervention.

The Wellhausen school, then, professes an absolute skepticism in regard to the Sacred Books which purport to give the history of the Chosen People. If the assertions of the first proponents of the critical school are to be accepted, the proto-history of the Hebrews takes us back to the most ancient period of mankind, a period for which we possess in their opinion no trustworthy sources. Need it be recalled here that in the course of the first half of the nineteenth century, it was stated on all sides that the

---

harmonize the conclusions of the critics with the principles of Catholic theology." It was his misfortune to live to see his star dimmed considerably, even from the purely critical viewpoint. See a résumé of his views on the history of Israel in his last book, *La Crise morale du Temps présent et l'Education humaine* (Paris, 1937), 20-24.

first historical works contemporaneous with the events they narrated were those of Herodotus († 408 B. C.)? At all events, it was added, historical literature was certainly of late origin in Israel. One was not allowed to refer, in support of the opposite opinion, to the fourteenth verse of the fifth chapter of Judges, for there not the pen of a scribe but the rod of authority is mentioned! Even elsewhere, some asserted, the course of ancient history cannot be traced back with any certitude beyond the sixth century. From the standpoint of history Greece was a land of privilege, and yet she was able to recall nothing historical previous to the age of Solon the lawgiver (594) and of Pisistratus (561-527). In Italy history made a difficult beginning with the capture of Rome by the Gauls in 390. For the Near East, the lands of the Fertile Crescent, where the children of Israel originated and where they finally settled, traditions possessing any worth are far rarer, they held, and less ancient. Herodotus and Diodorus of Sicily (first century B. C.), two great travelers before the face of the Eternal, gathered together not a few observations on the ancient Orient; and in addition, Flavius Josephus and Eusebius of Cæsarea have preserved a certain number of fragments of the ancient chroniclers: Ctesias (c. 360), Berosus (c. 300), and Manetho (c. 270). Little faith is to be put, however, in the information given by these authors. They gathered traditions and worked them up into a confused synthesis under the influence of sheer fancy or a nondescript philosophy of history. For if history is to be written from a philosophical viewpoint, as Voltaire maintained, it must not degenerate into mere philosophizing.

Even the writers of the Wellhausen school who considered the position of Israel as privileged, felt that its history begins with the Books of Samuel. Everything prior to the period of this judge defies, so to speak, historical investigation. The patriarchs belong to the realm of religious legend or perhaps even to mythology. The Mosaic traditions contain undoubtedly some grain of truth, but the person of Moses as well as the leading incidents of his career, and especially the happenings on Sinai, have been utterly misrepresented. For the historian, they held, the five books of Moses are an undecipherable hodgepodge. They can be read only with the eyes of faith.

In the second place, the liberal wing of the Wellhausen school clung to the scientific theory of evolution and applied to the Israelites the evolutional scheme elaborated by independent historians of the last century to explain the origin of all the civilizations of antiquity. From the viewpoint of social organization, the children of Israel, after having led a nomadic life and devoted themselves to cattle-raising, are presumed to have developed into a farming people and later into a nation of artisans and traders. Such an evolution from the simple to the complex must have characterized also the religious history of the Hebrews. From a compact mass of animistic and manistic, totemistic and fetishistic beliefs which defy inventory, there gradually emerged, through a succession of progressive refinements, the divine and transcendent figure of Yahweh. The primitive beliefs were arranged into a polydemonism which later evolved into a polytheism. In their turn, the polytheistic beliefs were transformed as manifold tendencies to henotheism gained the ascendency. The result was a monolatric religion, centered about

Yahweh, who successfully imposed himself on the allied tribes, becoming both a rallying cry and an inspirational force. Lastly, the prophetic preachers and writers of the ninth and eighth centuries are credited with the transformation of this Yahwistic religion into a strict moral monotheism, which remained forever after the glory of the ancient Hebrews. According to this opinion, the development of the ancient Israelite religion was accomplished in an almost direct line and was mainly the work of the eighth century. The prophets themselves thus become the religious geniuses to whom the people of Israel was indebted for the fine flower of its beliefs and institutions. Accordingly, Biblical tradition is erroneous and perhaps positively deceptive when it pictures the men of God of the ninth and eighth centuries as reformers trying to lead the Yahwistic religion back several centuries to the ideal conditions of the Mosaic era.

Finally, liberal and rationalistic Wellhausenism denied the reality of any supernatural intervention in the origin or development of the religion of Israel. It held for the total immanence of the process which called forth the marvelous unfolding of Hebrew prophetism and monotheism. Here particularly does thoroughgoing rationalistic Wellhausenism come face to face with serious historical difficulties, especially when it has to explain why, of all the divinities of the ancient East, Yahweh alone, the god of the Hebrews, became a transcendent, moral, universal Deity, the sole God of the universe. Such a destiny did not fall to the lot of Marduk, Assur, Kamos, Mèlèk, or any other divinity, even though more powerful or better favored by historical circumstances.

For want of a more satisfactory theory, many critics accept the explanation of Karl Budde. According to him, Yahwism was the only religion to become rigidly monotheistic, universal, and missionary, because in this case alone the god to whom it directs its adoration was voluntarily chosen from the outset by his devotees after a freely concluded bilateral covenant. Undoubtedly Yahweh, too, was of old a nature god with a purely local renown. Perhaps he was the tribal god of the Kenites. It was not as a nature divinity, however, that he became the god of Israel. This happened as a consequence of the alliance of Sinai, whereby Yahweh acquired among his people, not the limitless and untrammeled power of brute force, but rather royal power — constitutional power, one might say, resting fundamentally on the notions of alliance, of mutual rights and duties. In other words, at the base of Yahwism there is not the working of vague, blind forces; there is a choice, an election, a legal contract, one of those profoundly human acts, free and deliberate, which are the foundation of mankind's moral life.[39]

Upholders of Wellhausen's literary conclusions who at the same time kept their faith and opposed religious liberalism — Eduard König was once their leading spokesman — maintained that this rationalistic explanation is false.[40] Was Yahweh in reality, they asked, the tribal god

---

39. Some of these views, modified in the light of the progress in critical studies, will be found again in Eerdmans, *De Godsdienst van Israël* (Huis-ter-Heide [Utrecht], n.d. [1930]), 2 vols.

40. E. König, *Geschichte des Reiches Gottes bis auf Jesus Christus* (Berlin, 1908) ; *Geschichte der alttestamentlichen Religion kritisch dargestellt* (2nd ed., Gütersloh, 1915) ; *Theologie des Alten Testaments kritisch und vergleichend dargestellt* (Stuttgart, 1922) ; *Die messianischen Weissagungen des Alten Testaments, vergleichend, geschichtlich und exegetisch behandelt* (Stuttgart, 1923). On König (1846-1936), see *Ephemerides Theologicæ Lovanienses,* XIV (Louvain, 1937), 407.

of the Kenites? By what right can it be pretended that Yahweh was freely chosen by the children of Israel? Rather, must not the contrary be asserted? If the Hebrews clung to Yahweh, it was because Yahweh took the initiative by choosing them and reserving them for Himself as His chosen people. Even supposing that the choice did come in the first instance from Israel and not from Yahweh, is it fitting to interpret it as inspired solely by considerations of an ethical nature? Moreover, even granted the fact, the problem remains unsolved. How explain the ethical character of this choice, an unparalleled phenomenon in the religious history of the ancient Orient? How attribute to this ethical factor a potency capable of transforming by magical metamorphosis a naturalistic Kenite god into the moral and transcendental God of Moses and the Israelites? All this helps us to understand why Christian exegetes, who were convinced that they had to adopt a certain number of Wellhausen's literary conclusions, did not cease to combat the rationalistic views held by the same school in the matter of religious history.

B. *The Critico-literary Conclusions of the Wellhausen School:*

The chief critico-literary conclusion of Wellhausenism — and this may be considered the pivotal point of the system — was the reversal of the chronological order of the books of the Law and the prophetical writings. While a virtually unanimous tradition affirms the five books of Moses to be the most ancient documents of Hebraic literature, and consequently to antedate the prophets, the school of Wellhausen puts off the solemn promulgation of the Law until after the Babylonian Exile and places the composition of the principal codes at the earliest after the great prophetical movement. Only the Book of the Covenant and, possibly, the most ancient editing of the Yahwistic and Elohistic narrative sections could by this interpretation go back further than the eighth century. Instead of appearing as restorers of Mosaic monotheism, which the present order of the books of the Bible shows them to be, the prophets are represented as the first to build up and preach the idea. A daring literary fraud attributing its origin to Moses thus made him the great law-giver of the Hebrews and the founder of the religion which is the incomparable achievement of the people of Israel.[41]

A more detailed statement is now in order of the views of the Wellhausen school on the various categories of books which make up the Holy Scriptures.

First of all, in the case of the HISTORICAL BOOKS, the followers of Wellhausen consider it proper to study the first six books of the Bible as a unit. They accordingly suggest the substitution of the term Hexateuch for the traditional Pentateuch.[42] In these books critical writers profess to sense the presence of four written sources, perfectly distinct though closely interwoven: the Yahwist, the Elohist, the Deuteronomist, and finally the Priestly Code or *Priestercodex*. They hold this to be especially true of Genesis, Exodus, and Josue. Each of the source-documents is supposed to be made up of narrative and statutory sections and most of them are thought to admit of being further broken up into several sources, or at least

41. Duhm, *Die Theologie der Propheten.*
42. See Steuernagel's imposing critical *Introduction* to the Old Testament, *Lehrbuch der Einleitung in das Alte Testament.*

to give evidence of several editings. The chronological succession of the four documents may be represented as follows: the starting point is the *Bundesbuch* or Book of the Covenant (Exodus xx, 23-xxiii, 19), a code of laws which has been connected with the sanctuary of Bethel and which is thought to have been composed about 870 B. C. Then follow the narrative sections which give the Yahwistic and Elohistic accounts of the origins of Israel, written respectively about 850 and 770, and consequently under the influence of the most ancient prophetical preaching. These accounts are supposed to have been combined into a single historical work at about 680 during the reign of Manasses. Half a century later, about 631, would come the composition of the second important collection of Hebraic law, namely, that which forms chapters xii to xxvi of Deuteronomy. The success of these new laws was so remarkable because of the pious fraud to which in 621 the priests of Jerusalem had recourse in order to win for Yahweh the good will shown by King Josias toward the Holy City and its Temple. The sponsors of the Deuteronomical reform added several prologues and epilogues, a setting retained even to this day. Then they revised the Yahwistic annals of Israel to bring them into accord with their ideas on the philosophy of religious history. The Babylonian Exile (597 and 587), coming unexpectedly about thirty years after the reform of Josias, made imperative a new revision of the Torah. The first to try his hand at it was the prophet Ezechiel. His plans are at the base of the sacerdotal legislation which begins with the Minor Law of Holiness, *Heiligkeitsgesetz* (Leviticus xvii-xxvi), and which finally resulted in the promulgation of the complete

Torah, a project realized about 445 through the reforming activity of Nehemias and Esdras.[43]

The general conclusion, then, is that the Laws of
Moses reflect in the main three literary agencies, the
prophetical schools of the ninth and eighth centuries, the
Deuteronomical reformers, and the sacerdotal groups of
the Babylonian Exile and succeeding years. These same
influences were brought to bear on the historical books,
and the critics accordingly distinguish a triple history of
the beginnings of Israel — the most ancient, called the
prophetical; then, the Deuteronomical; and finally, the
priestly or sacerdotal. The last-mentioned marshals the
facts around the four covenants which marked the com-
munications of God with mankind, the covenants of
Elohim with Adam, Noe, Abraham, and Moses.

When critical studies were beginning, the conclusions
on the WRITINGS OF THE PROPHETS were of a less revolutionary character. The predecessors of Wellhausen were
usually satisfied with casting doubt on the authenticity of
Micheas iv-vii, Isaias xl-lxvi, and Zacharias ix-xii. The
entrance of Bernhard Duhm and Julius Wellhausen
into the discussion caused the overthrow of the old positions. Wellhausen's commentary on the twelve minor
prophets is significant since it shows clearly the workings
of the radical virus which was later to cause the decline of
the school. In his analysis of the text, he notes the presence of a number of additions to the primitive prophecies.
It is a matter not only of glosses or interpolations but of
entire sections which have changed the character and

---

43. For the details of these various solutions, read the *Introductions*
of Cornill and Steuernagel. With these compare E. Sellin, *Einleitung in
das Alte Testament,* Evangelisch-Theologische Bibliothek Series (Leipzig,
1929); trans., *Introduction to the Old Testament* (London, 1923).

meaning of the original. In general, these alterations of the text may be classified under two headings: some adapt the old prophecies to the Judean outlook and to a historical conception favoring the kingdom of Juda; others, and these are more numerous, insert Messianic and optimistic eschatological pericopes. These additions to what was primitively a message of woe reflect the preoccupation of post-Exilic prophetism with preaching happiness which the Lord would bestow upon His elect at the end of time. Wellhausen's analysis of the prophetical literature won the full approval of such rivals as Bernhard Duhm in Germany and Thomas Kelly Cheyne in England.[44]

As for the DIDACTIC BOOKS of the Old Testament, the critical school was almost unanimous in placing the composition of the major portion of them after the Babylonian Exile. The Book of Psalms was linked with the liturgy of the Second Temple, the building of which was begun in the second year of Darius I (519) and completed in his sixth year, that is, the third day of the month of Adar, 515. The most beautiful poems of the Psalter were held to be luscious fruits of post-Exilic piety — a piety essentially individualistic and free of the nationalistic and mundane limitations of classical Yahwism. Other Psalms of a more national appeal were assigned to the age of the Maccabees, a period of national revival centering about the Hasmonean dynasty. At that high point of patriotic exaltation, the princes Simon Maccabeus (143-135), John Hyrcanus (134-104), Aristobulus (104), and Alexander Janneus (104-76) so completely united in their per-

---

44. See an exposition of the critical viewpoint on the twelve minor prophets in Coppens, *Le chanoine Albin Van Hoonacker*, 78-81.

sons the political and religious hopes of the nation that
an unknown writer is supposed to have proclaimed Simon
the king-priest established forever by Yahweh Himself on
Mount Sion.[45]

The strictly SAPIENTIAL BOOKS were also considered.
Job was assigned, without much dispute, to the period of
the Exile or immediately after it. The other books seemed
to have been influenced to an ever-increasing extent by
Greek philosophy and consequently their definitive composition would necessarily have taken place during the
Hellenistic period. There was no reason, however, why
the beginnings of Israelite wisdom should not be put back
to pre-Exilic times, and even to the eighth and seventh
centuries.[46]

We are justified therefore in concluding that the
Wellhausen reconstruction of Hebraic literary history distinguishes three periods of activity corresponding to as
many religious reform movements. First comes the ancient
prophetical literature, with its predictions of prosperity
and Messianic visions eliminated, and with moral instruction and visions of national disaster accentuated. The
progressive compilation of the various codes forming the

---

45. The theory of the Maccabean origin of the Psalms was upheld
in recent years most vigorously by R. H. Kennett (1864-1932), in his
Old Testament Essays (Macmillan, 1928). Read S. A. Cook's Introdu-
tion to Kennett, *The Church of Israel: Studies and Essays* (Cambridge,
1933), xlix. See M. Buttenwieser, "Are There Any Maccabean Psalms?" in
Journal of Biblical Literature, XXXVI (1917), 225-248; and E. Goossens,
Die Frage nach makkabäischen Psalmen (Münster in Westphalia, 1914).

46. In this connection compare the discreet attitude of Abraham
Kuenen, *De Godsdienst van Israël*, I (1869), 388-391, 455-463; English
translation, *The Religion of Israel to the Fall of the Jewish State* (1874-
5), 3 vols., by A. H. May. The author cites the remark of Renan, "La
vérité est dans les nuances." Renan dates the codification of the most
ancient sapiential literature from the time of the "men of Hezekiah"; he
argues that it derived simultaneously from Israel and Judah. (*History
of the People of Israel*, London, Chapman and Hall, 1891, III, 57-78).

Torah is the second period's contribution, although it is admitted that some elements of this literature, notably the Book of the Covenant, are contemporaneous with the ancient prophecies. Besides, this legislative activity was accompanied by a revival of prophetical literature with Jeremias and Deutero-Isaias as its most representative writers. The DEVOTIONAL (*piétiste*), SAPIENTIAL, and APOCALYPTIC LITERATURES are supposed to have developed last of all, with the Psalter, Job, and Daniel as the best representatives of these categories.

This sketch shows that the literary conclusions of the critical school, far from being opposed to the reconstruction of the religious history of Israel as elaborated by Vatke, von Bohlen, George, Reuss, Graf, and Wellhausen himself, strengthened it notably. Thereafter the books of the Old Testament, mounted in new settings and numbered according to a modified chronology, were found to be in agreement with the deductions of historical science and on this account acquired new value in the eyes of independent historians. After all the Old Testament was saved! Use of the books for the periods to which they purported to refer was, of course, not to be thought of for a moment. Yet their value as witnesses was not entirely destroyed. It sufficed to submit them to a good critical analyst who would bring out the true lineaments of their testimony and then, reversing the picture as in a magic lantern, would put them in a new historical perspective. So the adherents of Wellhausenism marched out in front of the moderates and conservatives, chanting a hymn of victory. To them the price paid for the preservation of the old documents did not seem excessive. They were proud of having proved that the books of the Old

Testament were not opposed to the inevitable historical criticism of themselves, but rather were found, if read through the eyes of the new school, to be in complete agreement with it. Wellhausen, personally, was so convinced of the excellence of his workmanship that he decided to abandon the Old Testament definitely. One job well done, he ostentatiously devoted himself to a new task, that of applying his illuminating method to the New Testament. He planned to renew his success by the solution of another problem as intricate as that of the Pentateuch — the literary provenience of the Synoptic Gospels.

V. Development of the Critical School after Wellhausen

The history of the critical school since Wellhausen proves that his name is not to be added to the list of the prophets, at least not without reservations. Contrary to his predictions, the tasks of criticism have not been considered by his disciples as entirely completed. In all branches new analyses — and at the moment the writer has in mind only the researches undertaken according to the method of Wellhausen himself — have been made, and they have complicated the problems. Since, however, recent investigations have not led to any generally acceptable conclusions, Wellhausen's prophecy has not been entirely discredited. His system has not had to make way for another and better grounded general hypothesis.

In what concerns the Hexateuch, many critics have extended the scope of their investigations by including in their researches the Book of Judges and the Books of

Samuel (the Octateuch), and sometimes even the Books of Kings (Enneateuch).[47] This is, with some variation, the position adopted by Karl Budde (in 1890 and 1902), Immanuel Benzinger (1921), Rudolf Smend (1921), Gustav Hölscher (1923), and Otto Eissfeldt (1925). Furthermore, certain authors think that the four classic sources, J E D P, do not exhaust the sum total of the documents used by the compilers and editors of the Hexa-Enneateuch. The literary unity of the Yahwist document was the first of the four to be attacked. Karl Ilgen, Eberhard Schrader, and even Julius Wellhausen himself entertained doubts about the homogeneity of this source. The question was revived and decided in favor of a second Yahwist document, by Karl Budde (1883), Charles Bruston (1885), Rudolf Smend (1912), Walther Eichrodt (1916), Johannes Meinhold (1921), Heinrich Holzinger (1922), and Otto Eissfeldt (1922).[48] Then the hour of

---

47. Budde, *Die biblische Urgeschichte* (1883); *Die Bücher Richter und Samuel* (1890); "Richter und Josua," in *ZAW* (1887); I. Benzinger, "Jahvist und Elohist in den Königsbüchern des Alten Testaments," in *BWAT*, new ser. 2 (1921); Smend, "J E in den geschichtlichen Büchern des Alten Testaments," in *ZAW*, XXXIX, 181-217; G. Hölscher, "Das Buch der Könige, seine Quellen und seine Redaction," *Forschungen zur Religion und Literatur des Alten und Neuen Testaments* (Göttingen, 1923) 158-213; Eissfeldt, *Die Quellen des Richterbuches* (Leipzig, 1925); T. Klaehn, *Die sprachliche Verwandtschaft der Quelle K der Samuelisbücher mit der Quelle J des Hexateuchs* (Borna-Leipzig, 1914); L. Hylander, *Der literarische Samuel-Saul-Komplex (I Sam. I-XV) traditionsgeschichtlich untersucht* (Leipzig-Uppsala, 1932). This prolongation of the sources into the historical books is also supposed by S. Mowinckel, "Der Ursprung der Bileamsage," *ZAW*, VII (1930), 233-271.

48. E. Schrader, *Studien zur Kritik und Erklärung der biblischen Urgeschichte* (1883); Budde, *Die biblische Urgeschichte;* Charles Bruston, "Les deux jéhovistes [from Genesis to the First Book of Kings]," in *Revue de Théologie et de Philosophie* (1885); H. Gunkel, *Die Genesis übersetzt und erklärt* (1901); Smend, *Die Erzählung des Hexateuchs auf ihre Quellen untersucht* (1912); W. Eichrodt, "Die Quellen der Genesis von neuem untersucht," in *BZAW*, 31 (1916); H. Holzinger, "Genesis, Exodus, Leviticus, und Numeri," in Kautzsch, *Heilige Schrift*

the Elohist document sounded. Doubts were formulated, timidly at first by Abraham Kuenen,[49] but developed *ex professo* by Otto Procksch (1906). The dismemberment of Deuteronomy was pushed to the limit by Carl Steuernagel and Johann Hempel.[50] As for the Priestly Code, since its perfect unity had never been vigorously supported, the exegetes had only to stress the divisions and cuttings already introduced by the early proponents of criticism. The Law of Holiness (Leviticus xvii-xxvi) owes its existence as a literary unit especially to Karl Heinrich Graf and August Klostermann, the latter of whom designated it *Heiligkeitsgesetz*.

In 1912, Rudolf Smend attempted to formulate the results of post-Wellhausen research and of his own inves-

---

des Alten Testaments (Tübingen, 1922), and previously in *Einleitung in den Hexateuch* (Freiburg in Breisgau, 1893), 138-160; Eissfeldt, *Hexateuch-Synopse. Die Erzählung der fünf Bücher Moses und des Buches Josua mit dem Anfange des Richterbuches in ihre vier Quellen zerlegt und in Deutscher Uebersetzung dargeboten* (Leipzig, 1922); Meinhold, "Die jahvistischen Berichte in Gen. 12-50," in *ZAW*, XXXIX (1921), 42-57; J. W. Rothstein, "Die ältere Schicht in der jahv. Ueberlieferung der Urgeschichte," in *BZAW*, 39 (1921); Morgenstern, "The Oldest Document of the Hexateuch," in *Hebrew Union College Annual*, IV (Cincinnati, 1927).— The problem was recently reconsidered by Mowinckel, *The Two Sources of the Predeuteronomic Primeval History* [*J E*] *in Gen. 1-11* (Oslo, 1937). He sets aside the theory of a Second Yahwist for these chapters and discovers in the supposed Deutero-Yahwistic sections the presence of the Elohist.

49. Kuenen, *Historisch-critisch onderzoek naar het ontstaan en de verzameling van de Boeken des Ouden Verbonds,* I (1st and 2nd ed., Leyden, 1885); English translation, *An Historico-critical Inquiry into the Origin and Composition of the Hexateuch* (Macmillan, 1886), by Philip Wicksteed; O. Procksch, *Das nordhebräische Sagenbuch: Die Elohim-quelle* (1906). It should not be forgotten that originally the Priestly Code was called the Elohist, and what is now called the Elohist was then labeled the Second Elohist. The Priestly Code was discovered first and was long considered the more ancient document. In the present case, there is question of a Deutero-Elohist to be distinguished in the so-called Second Elohist itself.

50. The author has previously set forth the situation in regard to Deuteronomy in "Quelques publications récentes sur les Livres de l'Ancien Testament," *ETL*, XI (1934), 603-608.

tigations in a work of synthesis which suggested a new (the fourth) documentary theory for the Hexateuch.[51] Apart from Deuteronomy, Smend distinguished in the books attributed to Moses four documents, the First Yahwist, the Elohist, the Second Yahwist (which included supposed additions to J and E), and the Priestly Code. Not unlike this new solution are the theories of Walther Eichrodt, Heinrich Holzinger, Johannes Meinhold, and especially, Otto Eissfeldt. The better to indicate the special character of the new documentary theory, the last-mentioned author proposed a new name for the ancient Yahwist document, viz., *Laienquelle* or Lay Source. At the same time he proposed that the term Yahwist be reserved to the Deutero-Yahwist sections of the Hexateuch.[52]

In order to make this exposition as complete as possible, there should be added to these general studies a word on certain authors who postulate special sources for definite sections of the Mosaic books. For Genesis, reference may be made to the articles of Romanoff and Pfeiffer, and particularly to the monograph of Gerhard von Rad, who discerns all through Genesis the presence of two narrators of the priestly order.[53] As for the legislative sections, the

---

51. Smend, *Die Erzählung des Hexateuchs.* See Eissfeldt, *Hexateuch-Synopse,* 4.

52. See *supra,* note 48, and also Eissfeldt, *op. cit.,* 1-88. The latter recently summed up his stand in the article, "Pentateuch," in *Paulys Real-Enzyclopädie der Classischen Altertumswissenschaft.* Begonnen von G. Wissowa, herausgegeben von W. Kroll, new ed., 1st ser., *Pech bis Petronius,* XIX, 1 (1937), col. 513-524. The same author has just taken up the defense of the Second Elohist (or simply, the Elohist), the existence of which, as we shall see, was questioned by Rudolph and Volz in "Die Komposition von Exodos 1-12. Eine Rettung des Elohisten," id *Theologische Blätter,* XVIII (1939), 224-233.

53. R. H. Pfeiffer, "A Non-Israelite Source of the Book of Genesis," in *ZAW,* VII (1930), 66-73; P. Romanoff, "A Third Version of the Flood Narrative," in *JBL,* L (1931), 304-7; G. von Rad, *Die Priester-*

publications of Jepsen, Menes, and Morgenstern have
called into doubt even the conclusions that the Wellhausen
school had drawn on the composition of the Book of the
Covenant, conclusions that had been accounted among
the most certain.[54]

Finally, the important differences of opinion will be
indicated in regard to the relative and absolute chronology of the various legal codes admitted by the critical
school. It may be well to recall that the most widely
accepted relative chronology enumerates the documents
in the following order: the Yahwist, the Elohist,
Deuteronomy, the Minor Law of Holiness, and the major
portion of the dissected Priestly Code. This order
was commonly accepted, although distinguished writers
have questioned the position of the first two codes.
August Köhler, August Dillmann, and Eduard König, for
example, placed the Elohist at the head of the list.

Differences of opinion are more evident in the case
of the Priestly Code and Deuteronomy. Many exegetes
dispute the Wellhausen theory of the recent origin of all
the Deuteronomic or sacerdotal laws.

The absolute chronology has, however, undergone the
most serious changes. According to Wellhausen the starting point of this chronology is the year 621 during the

---

schrift im Hexateuch (Stuttgart, 1934); Mowinckel, "Hat es ein israeli-
tisches Nationalepos gegeben?" in *ZAW*, XII (1935), 130-152. See
Eissfeldt, "Modern Criticism," in *Rec. Rev.*, 76-8.

54. A. Jepsen, *Untersuchungen zum Bundesbuch,* Beiträge zur Wissenschaft vom Alten und Neuen Testament, 3rd ser., fasc. 5 (Stuttgart,
1927); A. Menes, "Die vorexilischen Gesetze Israels," in *BZAW*, 50
(1928); Morgenstern, "The Book of the Covenant," in *HUCA*, V
(1928), 1-151, VII (1930), 19-258, VIII-IX (1931-2), 1-150; Caspari,
"Heimat und Soziale Wirkung des altt. Bundesbuches," in *Zeitschrift der
deutschen morgenländischen Gesellschaft*, VIII (1929), 97-120; Pfeiffer,
"The Transmission of the Book of the Covenant," in *Harvard Theological
Review*, XXIV (1931), 99-110.

reign of King Josias when the "Torah of Moses" was discovered. Following the example of Leberecht de Wette
and Eduard Riehm, the disciples of Wellhausen identify
this code with Deuteronomy. Now this identification is
more and more being questioned; or, at least, many
authors who accept it provisionally still hold that
Deuteronomy was not composed at that time. Indeed, if
we are to admit the arguments of Adam C. Welch and
T. Oestreicher, the Deuteronomic code goes back to
Samuel's prophetic activity. Robert H. Kennett and
Gustav Hölscher, on the contrary, maintain that it dates
from the Exile or from the period of the Second Temple.
As a code of radical reform, it came to light among a
small group of idealists during or after the Exile; as a
moral and social code, it brings to a close the internal
evolution of Israelite Law.

According to Wellhausen's school the second fixed
date of the absolute chronology of the codes is the promulgation of the Priestly Code by Esdras and Nehemias in
445. Here again, several recent works maintain that the
accepted positions have been overthrown. Charles Cutler
Torrey and Sigmund Mowinckel have demolished bit by
bit the historical framework into which the Wellhausen
school fixed the solemn post-Exilic promulgation of the
Law.[55]

---

55. For the priority of the Elohist, see Dillmann, *Nu., Dt., Jo.*
(1886); E. König, *Einleitung,* 204-9; A. Köhler, *Lehrbuch der bibl.
Geschichte A. Ts.* (1875-1893), 2 vols. On the problem of Deuteronomy,
see Coppens, "Quelques publications récentes," in *ETL,* XI (1934), 603-8.
Add to the bibliography of that article the following studies: a) in
support of an Exilic date: G. R. Berry, "The Code Found in the Temple,"
in *JBL,* XXXIX (1920), 44-51; F. C. Burkitt, "The Code Found in the
Temple," *ibid.,* XL (1921), 166-7; Kennett, *Deuteronomy and the
Decalogue* (Cambridge, 1920), and "The Origin of the Book of Deuteronomy," in *The Church of Israel* (Cambridge, 1933), 73-98; b)

It has already been intimated in what direction the
study of PROPHETICAL LITERATURE evolved. Less sensational than that concerned with the Pentateuch, it reached
a more tangible result, namely, the discovery of a Trito-
Isaias, usually limited to chapters lvi-lxvi of the Book
of Isaias. Bernhard Duhm was the first, apparently, to
detect with exactness the differences which mark off these
chapters from other parts of the same book, and notably
from chapters xl-lv, the Book of the Consolation of
Israel. Exegetes, however, are far from being in agreement on the religious aspects of the Trito-Isaias, and consequently on the date of its composition. Some connect
these chapters with the period of the Exile, others assign
them to the years which witnessed the rise of the
Samaritan schism. If this latter hypothesis be admitted, it

in support of a post-Exilic date: Hölscher, "Komposition und Ursprung
des Deuteronomiums," in ZAW, XL (1922), 161-255; F. Horst, "Die
Kultusreform des Josia," in ZDMG, LXXVII (1923), 220-238; W.
Spiegelberg, "Zur Datierung des Deuteronomiums," in Orientalische
Literaturzeitung, XXVI (1923), col. 481-482; Caspari, "Weltreichbege-
benheiten bei den Deuteronomisten," ibid., XXVII (1924), 8-11; c)
in support of the Riehm-Wellhausen date: Eerdmans, "Deuteronomy,"
in Old Testament Studies (London, 1927), 77-84, and De Godsdienst
van Israël, I, 144-150. On the entire question, read Coppens, "La réforme
de Josias. L'objet de la réforme de Josias et la loi trouvée par Helcias,"
in ETL, V (1928), 581-598.

On the reform of Esdras and Nehemias: Torrey, Composition and
Value of Ezra-Nehemiah (Giessen, 1896); Ezra Studies (Chicago, 1910);
"The Chronicler's History of the Return under Cyrus," in American
Journal of Semitic Languages and Literatures, XXXVII (1921), 81-100.
Torrey states that I Erza iv, 43-v, 6 fills in the gap which many
exegetes had noted between Ezra I and II; the passage is from the
Chronicler's pen, and it relates the return of the Jews under Cyrus. This
conclusion had been attacked by J. A. Bewer, "The Gap between Ezra,
Chapters I and II," ibid., XXXV (1919), 18-26. — Mowinckel, 1.
Statholderen Nehemia. 2. Ezra den Skriftlaerde, Kristiania (1916);
Hölscher, "Les origines de la communauté juive à l'époque perse," in
RHPR, VI (1926), 105-126; A. Thomson, "An Inquiry concerning the
Books of Ezra and Nehemiah," in AJSL, XLVIII (1932), 99-132.

For works favoring the historicity of Esdras-Nehemias, read H. H.
Schaeder, Ezra der Schreiber (1930), and A. Van Selms, Ezra en Nehemia
(Groningen, 1935). The latter is an excellent little commentary.

has still to be decided whether the schism goes back to the time of Nehemias (445) or to that of Alexander the Great.[56]

In the course of these discussions, two other problems connected with the prophetical literature attracted attention. They concern the origin of Deutero-Isaias and the composition of the Book of Ezechiel. While the orthodox Wellhausen school hails the author of Isaias xl-lv as the prophet *par excellence* of the Exile, a certain number of critics place him later and consider him a writer of the land of Israel.[57] More radical than his predecessors, Wilhelm Caspari denies that the Deutero-Isaias is the literary production of one historical personage. He suggests that chapters xl-lv be interpreted as a collection of songs and poems of more or less identical inspiration and style which originated among the exiles and repatriates of 537, the record of their hopes and of the stages of their return journey to the Promised Land. As for Ezechiel, he had to submit to a dissection like that of which Isaias was the victim. Torrey and Hölscher have cut the book in two, crediting one half to an anonymous prophet who lived during the Exile, and the other half to a priest who exercised his ministry of reform after the repatriation of the Jews. These very uncertain opinions have not won the approval of many scholars. In a manner somewhat similar to that of Hölscher and Torrey,

56. L. E. Browne, *Early Judaism* (Cambridge, 1929). See Coppens, *Quelques publications récentes sur les Livres de l'Ancien Testament: Les livres prophétiques, le Psautier* (Bruges, Beyaert, 1935), 16.

57. Torrey, *The Second Isaiah: A New Interpretation* (Edinburgh, 1928). — See also J. A. Maynard, "The Home of Deutero-Isaiah," in *JBL*, XXXVI (1917), 213-224; and M. Buttenwieser, "Where Did Deutero-Isaiah Live?", *ibid.*, XXXVIII (1919), 94-112. The literary unity of the Deutero-Isaias has been discussed and denied by Caspari, *Lieder und Gottessprüche der Rückwanderer (Jesaja 40-55).*

Volkmar Herntrich and Canon John Battersby Harford have developed theories of dual authorship.[58]

The other prophetical books have for the most part escaped critical dissection. Torrey's attempt to dismember the Book of Jeremias proved unsuccessful. Budde and Mowinckel made efforts to reconstruct the primitive source of the Proto-Isaias, but their results were too subjective to be received with enthusiasm. The relationship between the Deutero- and Trito-Isaias fascinates many exegetes, but up to the present they have not agreed on a solution. Finally, though some progress has been made in the exegesis of the Book of Daniel by study of its language and historical background, the common opinion has not shifted noticeably.[59] Since the beginning of the last century critics have looked upon this book as a production of the age of the Maccabees.

There is little progress to note in the critical study of DEVOTIONAL and SAPIENTIAL LITERATURE. The conclusions of Wellhausen are retained almost in their entirety. At most, one writer or another broaches opinions of a more radical nature. Robert H. Kennett, for instance, suggests an exclusively Maccabean origin for the book of Psalms.[60]

---

58. Hölscher, *Geschichte der israelitischen und jüdischen Religion, Die Theologie im Abriss* ser. (Giessen, 1922); Torrey, *Pseudo-Ezekiel and the Original Prophecy* (New Haven, 1933); "Certainly Pseudo-Ezekiel," in *JBL*, LIII (1934), 291-320. On the alleged recent date of several sections of Ezechiel, read Berry: "The Authorship of Ezekiel," *ibid.*, XXXIV (1915), 17-40; "The Date of Ezekiel, 45, 1-8ª, and 47, 13-48, 35," *ibid.*, XL (1921), 70-75; "The Date of Ezekiel, 38, 1-39, 20," *ibid.*, XLI (1922), 224-232. Read also V. Herntrick, "Ezekiel-probleme," in *BZAW*, 61 (1932); and J. Battersby Harford, *Studies in the Book of Ezekiel* (Cambridge, 1935).

59. Read *Rec. Rev.*, 95-8, and W. Baumgartner, "Ein Vierteljahr-hundert Danielforschung," in *Theologische Rundschau*, XI (1939), 59-83, 125-144, 201-228.

60. See *supra*, notes 45 and 46.

Of the works cited up to this point, few deal with the HISTORY OF ISRAEL in its entirety, and none of them looks to the substitution of an original historical synthesis for the one which made Wellhausen such a success. The publications of Smend and Eissfeldt, which certainly rank among the most important, take account only of the Hexateuch, and, what is more, they do not modify classic Wellhausenism substantially.

An exception must, perhaps, be made for the work of the Scotchman, Adam C. Welch, and the American, C. C. Torrey, provided one takes the trouble to extract a general theory from their numerous publications.[61]

Welch, a firm believer in the critico-literary method, has recently completed a four-volume synthesis on the origin of the Israelites. The work is impressive and merits

---

61. A. C. Welch: *The Religion of Israel under the Kingdom* (Edinburgh, 1912) ; *Visions of the End: A Study in Daniel and Revelation* (London, 1922) ; *The Code of Deuteronomy: A New Theory of Its Origin* (London, 1924) ; "The History of Israel," in *The People and the Book; Deuteronomy: The Framework of the Code* (London, 1932) ; *Post-Exilic Judaism* (London, 1935) ; *Prophet and Priest in Old Israel* (London, 1936). A new book by Welch is announced: it will treat of the Chronicles, and will be issued in the Schweich Lectures series (London).

Torrey: *Composition and Historical Value of Ezra-Nehemiah; Ezra Studies; The Second Isaiah: A New Interpretation; Pseudo-Ezekiel and the Original Prophecy.* For a summary of Professor Torrey's views, see his *The Second Isaiah,* 28-31, and especially *Pseudo-Ezekiel,* 192-8.

Along with these two exegetes should also be mentioned as among the authors who have left the beaten track and are tending toward a new historical synthesis: E. Sellin, S. Mowinckel, F. Dornseiff, and G. von Rad. They will fit more properly into the following chapter. Von Rad still follows the Wellhausen tradition, as he shows in *Die Priesterschrift im Hexateuch* (Stuttgart, 1934) ; however, in *Das formgeschichtliche Problem des Hexateuchs, BWANT,* 4th ser., fasc. 26 (Stuttgart, 1938), he gives indications of taking to new paths.

In conclusion, the quite extraordinary position of E. Naville should be mentioned, merely as a curiosity. He postulates the existence of a Mosaic Pentateuch in Accadian and of a prophetical literature in Aramaic. See his *Archæology of the Old Testament: Was the Old Testament Written in Hebrew?* (London, Robert Scott, 1913) ; and *The Text of the Old Testament,* Schweich Lectures, 1915 (London, 1916).

serious examination by some younger scholar. Starting
with the history of Israel under the kings and with an
analysis of Deuteronomy, Welch has continued his investigation with the study of post-Exilic Judaism and the
levitical priesthood. This original synthesis, a conscien-
tiously built-up piece of work, proclaims the antiquity of
Deuteronomy, the preponderant rôle played by prophets
of the Northern Kingdom in the various religious reforms
(principally in that of Josias), the antiquity of part of
the Priestly Code, and the influence of Samaria during the
post-Exilic period.

The work of Torrey is much more individualistic,
and also much less objective. It is founded for the most
part on the hypothesis of an enormous literary fraud, consisting in the fabrication of several documents which
aimed at creating belief in the reality of a general
Babylonian Exile, in several returns under Darius, Cyrus,
and Artaxerxes II, and in the dominant rôle played by
these imaginary repatriates in the reconstruction of "post-
Exilic" Judaism. According to Torrey, this Judaism is the
work of a few groups of Judean reformers. They lived in
Palestine and held aloof from political disturbances in
order to work out, as a reaction against the nationalistic
Yahwism of "pre-Exilic" times, a spiritual Judaism from
which the Jewish "church" afterward arose. This reformed Judaism had to struggle, of course, against the
orthodox tradition. Torrey's really paradoxical hypothesis
represents, as the principal upholders of tradition, the
northern Israelites located at the time near Samaria — in
other words those who, once the battle was lost, became in
the eyes of the new orthodoxy the execrable Samaritans.
To justify their pretensions, the Judean reformers are said

to have sought to win the credence of the people by forging the legend of their glorious origin. To authorize their program of reform, they are supposed to have boasted of the purity of their stock and to have proclaimed themselves the one-hundred-percent descendants of the exiles of 587 and of the repatriates of 537. In this manner they were able to glorify their work as the spiritual heritage of the "pilgrim fathers," who by their noble courage and sufferings had preserved intact during the "Exile" the purity both of the seed of Abraham and of the Law of Moses. This enormous falsification of history led directly to the myth of the Babylonian Exile, to the interpolation of the Deutero-Isaias, and to the complete remodeling of the prophecies of Ezechiel. It finds its pseudo-historical expression in the Chronicles and the Books of Esdras and Nehemias, while the echoes of the violent struggles between the Judean reformers and the Samaritans resound in the incongruous fragments of the Trito-Isaias.

Like that of Welch, the work of Torrey did not make a deep impression. It has, however, received more attention from the critics. Ernest Sellin has discussed it and Sigmund Mowinckel has been influenced by it to an appreciable extent.

Conclusion

A cursory glance at the array of post-Wellhausen publications reveals two striking characteristics: first, the tendency, which at times degenerates into sheer fantasy, to dissect and parcel out the books of the Bible far more extensively than the first disciples of Wellhausen allowed; second, the lack of agreement among these critics. None of their findings, if we except the Trito-Isaias, has been incorporated into all the *Introductions* to the literature of the Old Testament. In short, while stressing once again that all the predictions of Wellhausen have not been verified, it must be admitted that the publications inspired by his methods continue to give the impression that the general lines of his imposing historical edifice are of solid construction. Such is the opinion expressed in a recent article by Mr. W. F. Lofthouse whose view may be summed up substantially as follows: "The triumph of the theory of Wellhausen may be said to have been gained, in England, with the publication of Sanday's Bampton lectures on *Inspiration,* delivered in Oxford in 1892, following Driver's *Introduction to the Literature of the Old Testament* (first edition, 1891). Since then, there has been no serious opposition in quarters where opposition was likely to count for much; and all subsequent Old Testament study, far from shaking that theory, has found that it could only proceed by making the Wellhausen view its starting-point and presupposition. . . . Indeed, the Wellhausen position may well be called orthodox. . . . Outside the Wellhausen propositions, any view of the history (to say nothing of the evolution) of Old Testament literature is so uncertain, that no conception of the evolution of religion can be founded on it."[62]

---

62. W. F. Lofthouse, "The Evolution of Religion in the Old Testament," in *The Modern Churchman,* XXIV (1934), 259-274, especially 259.

CHAPTER TWO

RECENT DEVELOPMENTS

IN THE first chapter an attempt was made to give a faithful account of the researches into the literary origins of the Bible which were undertaken in the course of the last century. The author endeavored to determine the guiding principles, to call attention to the principal works, to point out the results achieved by the masters and their disciples, and to indicate how this research has continued down to our own day. He also suggested that the vagaries and personal caprice of certain critics compromised in no small measure the system of the masters.

The boldness of conjecture and expression characteristic of hypercriticism was not the only factor which weakened the prestige of the Wellhausen school. In addition several more or less rival systems appeared. These accepted the principles and results of their predecessors in some matters but proposed radical changes in others, and in particular advocated new methods of investigation and synthesis. These innovations were developed simultaneously in different quarters.[1] As we shall see, it is not

---

1. The literature is copious. The author limits himself to a few books and articles which seem most suggestive: H. Gressmann, "Die Aufgaben der alttestamentlichen Forschung," *ZAW*, new ser., I (1924), 1-33; W. Staerk, "Zur alttestamentlichen Literaturkritik. Grundsätzliches und Methodisches," *ibid.*, I, 34-74; Gunkel, "The Historical Movement in the Study of Religion," *Expository Times*, XXXVIII (1927), 532-6; R. Kittel, *Die Alttestamentliche Wissenschaft in ihren wichtigsten Ergebnissen dargestellt.* (5th ed., Leipzig, 1929); Noordtzij, *Het Probleem van*

easy to find a name for them or even to point out their chief exponents. The leaders were numerous, their squadrons heterogeneous, their tactics varied, the fields of battle scattered. Special attention may, however, be called to the historico-folklorist school and to the importance of the rôle played by Hermann Gunkel[2] and Hugo Gressmann,[3] two exceptionally enterprising exegetes whose names will always be associated.[4]

Chapter one of this book analyzed what may be called classical Wellhausenism. An effort will be made in this chapter to present in the same way the principal

het Oude Testament; G. H. Van Senden, "Een paar opmerkingen over Professor Noordtzij's Dies-rede," *Nieuw Theologisch Tijdschrift* (1927), 259-265; Eichrodt, "Hat die alttestamentliches Theologie noch selbstständige Bedeutung innerhalb der alttestamentlichen Wissenschaft?" *ZAW*, VI (1929), 83-91; J. Pedersen, "Die Auffassung vom Alten Testament," *ibid.*, VIII (1931), 161-182; H. Torczyner, "Das literarische Problem der Bibel," *ZDMG*, LXXXV (1931), 287-324; I. Zolli, "La teoria documentaria e la questione della Genesi," *La Rassegna Mensile di Israel*, X (1935), 1-10 (also published separately). For English-speaking readers three valuable collections of essays are to be especially noted among non-Catholic publications: *The People and the Book, Record and Revelation,* and *The Haverford Symposium.*

From the Catholic viewpoint: A. Bea, "Biblische Kritik und neuere Forschung," *Stimmen der Zeit*, CXIV (1928), 401-412 — an article written not without a certain measure of enthusiasm; J. Levie, "La crise de l'Ancien Testament," *Nouvelle Revue Théologique*, LVI (1929), 818-839; the present author's various bulletins devoted to recent Scriptural studies: 1) *Quelques publications récentes sur les Livres de l'Ancien Testament* (Bruges, Beyaert, 1934); 2) *Les Livres prophétiques: Le Psautier* (1935); 3) *En marge de l'Histoire sainte* (Bruges, 1936); 4) *Chronique d'Ancien Testament* (1939).

The following are among the best for bibliographical lists: a) current bibliography — for the Bible: *Biblica* (Istituto Pontificio Biblico); for the Ancient East: *Archiv für Orientforschung* (Berlin); for the classical world: *Philologische Wochenschrift* (Leipzig, O. R. Reisland); b) selected current bibliography: *Theologische Revue* (Münster in Westphalia); *ETL* (Louvain); c) retrospective analytical bibliography: *ZAW* (Berlin); d) analytical and systematic bibliography: *Biblische Zeitschrift* (Paderborn); e) critical notices: *Revue biblique* (Paris-Jerusalem).

2. Hermann Gunkel (1862-1932), professor at Göttingen, Halle, Berlin, Giessen and Halle.

3. Hugo Gressmann (1877-1927), professor at Kiel and Berlin.

4. *ETL*, V (1928), 194-5, and IX (1932), 571-4.

schools which made it their business to rewrite the history of the Old Testament by studying the setting of events and ideas which prepared for it and helped to bring it into being. This second panel of this volume's projected triptych will be, if the reader cares so to imagine it, the central picture. It is no less instructive than the first, and it is equally necessary for the modest purpose of taking stock of critical studies and selecting from them a few guiding principles for Biblical exegesis and for the historiography of the Chosen People.

I. Leading Reactions against Classical Wellhausenism

In the foregoing exposition of the activities of the Wellhausen school, a primary importance in the elaboration of critical hypotheses was attributed to three factors: the theory of evolution, and the systematic application of it made to the religious history of the Chosen People; the rudimentary, and in great part grossly erroneous, conceptions of historical method which the disciples of Wellhausen exhibited in writing of the peoples of antiquity, particularly of those of the Near East; and the prejudices arising from a singularly narrow critico-literary method, which professed the greatest veneration for written tradition and interpreted it hypercritically according to the axiom, "Quod non est in actis, non est in re" — "If it is not recorded, it did not occur." Now, it is precisely against these three positions that the last thirty years have witnessed a strong reaction, which has called into question the classical Wellhausen picture of the Old Testament and Jewish history. The author proposes to examine the new movements in more detail and to indicate the achievements of the new masters at the expense of the school they have superseded.

A. The first reaction to be mentioned concerns the principle of evolution as applied to religious history. The assurance with which the authors of the first theories of the history of religions claimed to have explained the origin of mankind's beliefs has been noted above. The animistic theory particularly found much favor with the rationalists; but later hypotheses based on totemism, magic, preanimism — to mention only the more important — enjoyed each their hour of acclaim. For each, Old Testament exegesis and the interpretation of the religious history of Israel had to be adapted anew.

Yet even though these theories differed radically, they all proclaimed unshakable faith in the rectilinear evolution of the spiritual life of the human race from primitive forms to the highest patterns of religious and moral perfection. They also unanimously agreed in attributing this ascent to a wonderful dynamism inherent in the human soul and nobly and tirelessly lifting mankind toward a more and more transcendent future. These fantasies have been dissipated in the course of the last thirty years. They were unable to withstand the strictures of historical ethnologists and the challenge of facts brought to knowledge by the study of the so-called primitive civilizations. Most recent researches show that it is false to assign to man a rectilinear evolution in religion. Periods of retrogression have succeeded ages of progress, crises of decline and decay have affected even the great eras of cultural advance, and nothing is less sustained by proof than the supposed religious and moral depravity which writers have liked to postulate as the starting point of the spiritual ascent of mankind.

Moreover, the very idea of evolution has been hotly disputed and its field of application rigorously circumscribed. Scholars versed in the philosophy of history have shown without difficulty that the theory does not apply to the development of ancient Israel. In order to be able to speak of evolution at all, they argue, a group of individuals or a body of organically interrelated institutions must first be postulated, and secondly, the evolving subject must be animated by an immanent principle which is potentially superior to the concrete forms of organization found at the starting-point of the evolutionary process. In the case of the history of Israel, these two conditions are found to be virtually absent. Those who affirm an evolutional process in that history do not explain its motivating force; moreover, they postulate it for a conglomeration of beliefs and institutions having no vital connection and consequently offering no possibility of simultaneous development.

The evolutionistic theories are also proved to be inadequate by concrete *a posteriori* argument. None of them has succeeded in demonstrating absolutely that any of the primitive religious systems required for the evolutional process really existed at the beginning of the religious ascent of the Israelites. Attemps have been made to work back to an original manism, animism, totemism, or some other system, but in each case the verdict of facts has made it necessary to take refuge in new positions.[5]

---

5. Among believing exegetes who have successfully refuted the fantastic opinions of a certain school of comparative history of religions may be cited E. König (*Geschichte der alttestamentlichen Religion*) and

B. More effective still was the reaction against the Wellhausen system from the standpoint of the history of ancient Israel and the Near East. According to the followers of Wellhausen, Israel makes its appearance in the history of the world as an ancient and isolated people: an assertion which seems definitely to contradict the best established facts. To prove this, reference need only be made to the archæological research undertaken throughout the Near East. Its findings completely undermine the theory. It is proposed here to trace an outline sketch of what the archæologists have accomplished. Only the important facts will be noted.[6]

It is not excessive to make the general assertion that archæological excavations carried on in the Near East since the beginning of the nineteenth century have rescued from oblivion the civilization of peoples whose very names had all but disappeared from history. Archæologists have been able to penetrate into the heart of the ancient culture of Egypt, Assyro-Babylonia, and Phœnicia-Palestine. They have also resurrected the Sumerians, Hittites, Mitannians, Hurrians, Louites, Cassites, and Ugaritians — all hitherto almost unknown to history. And the complete list of these new peoples has not yet been definitely established.

F. X. Kortleitner. See Coppens, "Ancien Testament," *Apologétique,* ed. Maurice Brillant and Abbé Nédoncelle (Paris, 1937), 1080-89.

Recent authors in general have become more circumspect in the matter. See, for example, Oesterley-Robinson, *Hebrew Religion: Its Origin and Development* (2nd ed., London, 1937) ; E. Dhorme, *L'évolution religieuse d'Israël: I. La religion des Hébreux nomades* (Brussels, 1937) ; and particularly T. J. Meek, *Hebrew Origins* (New York, 1936).

6. The author has drawn extensively upon the excellent study of W. F. Albright, "How Well Can We Know the Ancient Near East?", *Journal of the American Oriental Society,* LVI (1936), 121-144. The best up-to-date bibliography is given in *AfO,* (Berlin, 1926 —). Since 1933, the Dutch Oriental Society, Ex Oriente Lux, has been publishing annuals which in the last few years have assumed large proportions. They are a good guide in the various Oriental fields.

Let us consider the principal advances of scientific Orientalism in the distinct, but related, fields of archæology and linguistics.[7] Egypt was the first land of the ancient East to be explored systematically. The first great expeditions, that of the French in 1798 and that of the Prussians in 1842, are well known. After 1836 there was an almost uninterrupted series of expeditions; by 1866, Lepsius, Brugsch, Birch, de Rougé, and Chabas had carried out explorations in the land of the Pharaos. A century has passed since the appearance of the first archæological albums — those of Rosellini (1832-1842), Wilkinson (1837-1841), and Tylor (1838). Between 1849 and 1859 Lepsius published his monumental collection, *Denkmäler aus Aegypten und Nubien.*

The carelessness with which the first explorers conducted their researches is common knowledge, but criticism should be tempered by reflection on the facts. They had to work under the worst possible conditions. The

7. H. Lamer, E. Unger, G. Venzmer, H. Härlin, *Schätze unterm Schutt: Mesopotamien, Aegypten, Griechenland, Rom* (Stuttgart, n. d. [1930]). The best popular albums are: H. Gressmann, A. Ungnad, H. Ranke, *Altorientalische Texte und Bilder zum Alten Testament* (Tübingen, 1909; 2nd ed., Berlin, 1926) ; *Cambridge Ancient History,* volume of plates, I, prepared by C. T. Seltman (Cambridge, 1927) ; L. Speleers, *Les Arts de l'Asie antérieure ancienne* (Brussels, 1926) ; G. Contenau, *Manuel d'archéologie orientale* (Paris, 1927). Marcel Brion gives a good popular treatment in *La résurrection des villes mortes: Mésopotamie, Syrie, Palestine, Égypte, Perse, Hittites, Crète, Chypre* (Paris, 1937). From the Biblical viewpoint: S. R. Driver, *Modern Research as Illustrating the Bible,* Schweich Lectures (London, 1909) ; Cook, *The Religion of Ancient Palestine in the Light of Archæology,* Schweich Lectures, 1925 (London, 1930) ; Hooke, "Archæology and the Old Testament," *Rec. Rev.,* 349-375; J. A. Montgomery, "The New Sources of Knowledge," *ibid.,* 1-27; A. Barrois, *Manuel d'archéologie biblique,* I (Paris, 1939).

No good handbook of texts and illustrations has been devised with a view to teaching the Bible. The work of L. Frohnmeyer and I. Benzinger, *Bilderatlas zur Bibelkunde* (Stuttgart, 1905), is poorly arranged and is today practically out of date because of the advances in Oriental science.

The first and best notices on current excavations are usually to be found in the *Illustrated London News.*

countries in which they toiled offered little security; the finances at their disposal were meager; their supplies of men and materials were limited. The technique of Eastern excavation was improved by Mariette (at work from 1850 onward) and by Sir Flinders Petrie, who was the first to employ in Egyptian chantiers (at Naucratis from 1880 to 1885) the methods which Schliemann had introduced about the year 1870 in Asia Minor. Greater perfection of technique was later achieved by Dörpfeld (1882), and still more recently by Koldewey and Reisner.[8]

Assyro-Babylonia was the second land of the Fertile Crescent to know a historical rebirth.[9] Here also two great expeditions sank spades into virtually virgin soil. In 1842, Botta, the French consul at Mosul, excavated on the site of Khorsabad, the ancient Dur-Sharrukin, built by Sargon the Assyrian at the end of the eighth century B. C. In 1845 the Englishman Layard explored the site of ancient Nineve — an expedition which led to the discovery of the library of King Assurbanipal. The most notable discoveries made here were included and described in the album published by Rawlinson. For the following years there should be mentioned the work of Ernest de Sarzec, who directed excavations at Tello, the ancient Lagash, and that of Jacques de Morgan, who discovered at Susa, capital of a kingdom bordering on ancient Babylonia, the triumphal stele of Naram-Sin (twenty-eighth century, B. C.) and the Code of Hammurabi (twenty-first century), the most important formulation of ancient law found up to the

---

8. J. A. Wilson, "The Present State of Egyptian Studies," *Haverford Symposium*, 202-224.

9. Meek, "The Present State of Mesopotamian Studies," *ibid.*, 158-187.

present time. Here, too, the system of Schliemann was adopted, this time by the German Koldewey. It was applied by Koldewey again at Babylon and Zenjirli, the ancient Sam'al, and by Andrae, Jordan, and Nöldeke at Assur and Erech-Warka. In its most perfect technical form — as achieved by Reisner — H. R. Hall, L. Woolley, H. Frankfort, J. Jordan, E. A. Speiser, A. Nöldeke, L. Watelin, R. Campbell Thompson, and M. E. L. Mallowan have found it a delicate instrument of archæological research. It is known what vast proportions the work assumed after the war of 1914-1918, when the peace of Versailles assured tranquillity and order in those distant regions, and English and American gold financed the caravans of the investigators. Let us recall: there were the excavations of Hall and Woolley at Ur, of Speiser at Kirkuk and Tepe Gawra, of Frankfort at Chafadje, Tell Agrab, and Tell Esmar, of von Oppenheim at Tell Halâf, of Jordan and Nöldeke at Uruk, of Woolley at Al Ubaid, of Mackay at Djemdet Nasr, of M. E. L. Mallowan at Tell Shagar Bazar, and of Barrois, Parrot and Dossin at Til-Barsib, Arslan-Tash, and Mari.[10]

Phœnicia made its entrance into this modern history of antiquity in the philological work of Gesenius (1786-1842) and in French archæological expeditions, the direction of which fell at one time into the hands of Ernest Renan. The discovery of the sarcophagus of Eshmun-Azar

---

10. Professor G. Dossin of the University of Liége recently stated that the archives of Mari are of vital interest to Biblists. The literature of Mari is supposed to contain matter likely to throw light on several points of Biblical Hebrew vocabulary. Zimrilim, the king of Mari whose correspondence has been found, is known to have been the contemporary of Hammurabi. On the excavations at Mari, see A. Parrot, *Villes enfouies: Trois campagnes de fouilles en Mésopotamie* (Paris, n. d. [1934]).

in 1856 was the most sensational event of those times, which already seem so distant. Since then, Phœnicia has yielded a few archæological and epigraphical documents of great importance, such as the sarcophagi and inscriptions of the kings, Akîrâm, Ahimilk, Abibaal, and Elibaal.[11]

It must be noted also how the Arameans, an ancient people well known to the Bible, make their appearance in the epigraphical history of the ancient East. A few texts have been unearthed, notably at Zenjirli, Afis, and Sujin-Sefire, which are of great value for the comparative study of Hebrew and for the problem of Aramaisms in Sacred Scripture.[12]

Of all the lands of the Fertile Crescent, Palestine was the last to be explored methodically.[13] Beginnings were difficult and discouraging. The first workers were sent out in 1865 by the Palestine Exploration Fund, and in 1877 by the *Deutscher Verein zur Erforschung Palästinas*. Before the First World War spades had unearthed, partially at least, a number of important tells, the sites of ancient Eglon (Tell-el-Hesi, formerly identified as Lachish), Gezer, Beth-Shemesh, Megiddo, Taanach, Jericho, Sichem, and Samaria. After the war, new chantiers were opened at Beth-Shan, Gerar, and on various tells not as yet iden-

---

11. See Montgomery, *Rec. Rev.*, 10; Albright, "The Present State of Syro-Palestinian Archæology," *Haverford Symposium,* 47-78.

12. See Montgomery, *loc. cit.*, 11-13; Fr. Rosenthal, *Die aramaistische Forschung seit Th. Nöldeke's Veröffentlichungen* (Leyden, 1939).

13. C. Watzinger, *Denkmäler Palästinas: Eine Einführung in die Archäologie des Heiligen Landes* (Leipzig, 1933-1935), 2 vols.; J. Simons, *Opgravingen in Palestina tot aan de Ballingschap (586 B. C.)* (Ruremonde, 1935); Kurt Galling, *Biblisches Reallexikon,* Handbuch zum Alten Testament ser. (Tübingen, 1934-1937); Albright, see note 11.

tified with certainty — Tell el-ful (the Gibe 'ah of Saul),
Tell en-Nasbeh (the Mizpah of Benjamin), Seilûn (the
Biblical Silo). These three localities are situated along the
road from Jerusalem to Sichem. Still later, work was begun at Tell Beit Mirsim (Kariath Sepher) on the road
from Beersheba to Jerusalem, and Tell ed-Duweir, the new
site of Lachish, on the road from Jerusalem to Gaza. Unfortunately, except for the so-called Letters of Lachish,
published by H. Torczyner,[14] these excavations have
yielded no written documents.

Although the soil of Palestine has been niggardly in
the matter of documents, light shines through the shadows
of prehistoric Palestine from three foreign sources. In
1887, the famous tablets containing the correspondence of
two Pharaos of the fifteenth century with their Palestinian
vassals were found at Tell el-Amarna, the city of
Amenophis IV, the great Egyptian heretic. These documents, the most valuable discovery treating of the Palestine
of pre-Exodus times, were published by 1896 by Hugo
Winckler.[15] Between 1901 and 1907 a second lot of documents treating of Israelite history, the famous Elephantine
papyri, was found in Egypt. This time it was the post-
Exilic period of Nehemias the Judean and Sanballat the
Samaritan that was revealed in new colors.[16] And now the
tablets of Ras Shamra-Ugarit, discovered in the mound of

---

14. Torczyner, *Lachish I (Tell ed-Duweir)*: *The Lachish Letters*
(London, Oxford University Press, 1938); Cf. Montgomery, *loc. cit.*, 23-5,
and D. W. Thomas, "The Lachish Letters," *Journal of Theological Studies*, XL (1939), 1-15. For the epigraphical texts of Palestine, consult the
compilation of David Diringer, *Le iscrizioni antico-ebraichi palestinesi*
(Florence, 1934).
15. J. A. Knudtzon, *Die El-Amarna Tafeln*, Vorderasiatische
Bibliothek, II (Leipzig, 1907-1910); standard edition, 1915.
16. Coppens, *Le chanoine Albin Van Hoonacker*, 53-67.

Ras Shamra between 1929 and 1933, promise us an abundant harvest of information on the period immediately preceding that of the Tell el-Amarna letters,[17] since these documents apparently are not later than the fifteenth century. What an unexpected windfall for the historians of ancient Palestine! They can now appeal to a set of authentic documents contemporaneous with the patriarchs.[18]

Although the reader may already feel submerged in a flood of discoveries, no mention has been made as yet of the results of excavations in lands bordering on the Fertile Crescent or connected with it by military, commercial, and cultural ties. India, Persia, Armenia, Asia Minor, Crete, Cyprus, and Arabia have their place in the picture; but a few hints will have to suffice here. Recent excavations in Arabia have brought to our knowledge various civilizations which appear in a far different light from that supposed in the *Reste arabischen Heidentums,* the celebrated manifesto of Wellhausen.[19] The Hittite archives of

---

17. Hans Bauer, *Die alphabetischen Keilschrifttexte von Râs Schamrá* in Lietzmann's Kleine Texte für Vorlesungen und Uebungen ser., no. 168 (Berlin, 1936). D. Nielsen, "Ras Samra Mythologie und Biblische Theologie," *Abhandl. für die Kunde des Morgenlandes,* XXI, 4 (Leipzig, 1936); R. Dussaud, *Les découvertes de Ras Shamra* (Ugarit) *et l'Ancien Testament* (Paris, 1937). These texts were first edited by C. Virolleaud (Paris, Geuthner). See Montgomery, 14-22, and Hooke, 353-358, both in *Rec. Rev.,* and especially the original and searching study of R. de Langhe, "Les textes de Ras Shamra-Ugarit et leurs apports à l'histoire des origines du peuple hébreu," *ETL,* XVI (1939), 245-327. This last has been separately reprinted.

18. The Proto-Sinaitic inscriptions might be mentioned along with the Amarna, Elephantine, and Ras Shamra texts. They are thought to be set down in an alphabet of great antiquity. Once they are deciphered correctly, they may prove to be very important for the history of ancient Egypt, Palestine, and Syria. The thirty odd characters employed in them invite comparison with the twenty-eight letters of the classical Arabic alphabet or the twenty-nine symbols of Southern Arabic. See Montgomery, *loc. cit.,* 6-7.

19. Montgomery, "The Present State of Arabian Studies," *Haverford Symposium,* 188-201.

Boghaz-Köi, discovered in 1906 by Hugo Winckler, have made imperative what we may without exaggeration call the historical resurrection of the Hittites.[20] Finally, important excavations in the prehistoric field were undertaken in the valley of the Indus by Sir John Hubert Marshall, in Baluchistan by Sir Aurel Stein, in Persia by Ernest Herzfeld, in Lybia by Leo Frobenius, in Egypt by Guy Brunton and Miss Caton Thompson, and in Palestine by Miss Dorothy Garrod, René Neuville, Père L. H. Vincent, Père Alexis Mallon, and F. Turville-Petre. As a result of these expeditions we know that the origin of the first civilizations of the Near East goes back beyond any definite reckoning.[21] Need it be noted that an enormous amount of work remains to be done in this field, and that we must prudently forego, for the present, any attempt to establish the points and means of contact of the cradles of prehistoric culture, reconstructed though they be with more or less verisimilitude?

A little late in getting started, the science of Oriental linguistics has followed the development of archæology.[22]

---

20. A. Götze, "The Present State of Anatolian and Hittite Studies," *ibid.*, 136-157.

21. See an attempt at fixing the chronology in Coppens, "Ancien Testament," *Apologétique* 1067-1070, based on Böhl, "Skizze der mesopotamischen Kulturgeschichte," *Nieuwe Theologische Studiën*, XXXVI (1936), 129-138. Cf. C. Lavergne, *Guide pratique de chronologie biblique* (Paris, 1937).

For the prehistoric East, see, besides the fundamental work of J. de Morgan and the great histories of the ancient East: C. U. A. Kappers, *An Introduction to the Anthropology of the Near East* (Amsterdam, 1934); V. Gordon Childe, *New Light on the Most Ancient East* (London, 1934); and *Man Makes Himself*, (New York, 1936).

22. Renan, *Histoire générale et système comparé des langues sémitiques: I. Histoire générale des langues sémitiques* (Paris, 1855); P. Dhorme, "Langues et écritures sémitiques," *Études sémitiques*, I (Paris, 1930); Thomas, *The Discovery of the Ancient Hebrew Language* (Inaugural Lecture, Cambridge, 1939); J. W. Flight, "The Present State of

The posthumous grammar of Champollion, published in 1836, was the first step toward mastery of the Egyptian language. After that, two contributions mark the rapid progress of the new science — the *Hieroglyphisch-demotisches Wöterbuch* of Brugsch (1867-1868, 1880-1882); and the first scientific grammar, Erman's *Neuägyptische Grammatik,* published in 1880. Perfection in lexicography and grammar was rapidly achieved in the studies of Erman, Sethe, Steindorff, and Grapow. The *Egyptian Grammar* of Gardiner, published in 1927, and the second edition of Erman's grammar (1933) have systematized the riches of Egyptological erudition which a century of learned research had produced.

Assyriology experienced more difficulty in breaking through its shell. Once on the scene, however, the new-born science enjoyed a robust constitution and excellent health. The language was deciphered about 1857, the year of the "contest" organized by the Asiatic Society of London, and the institution of the great German school of Assyriology followed. Schrader laid its foundations, and Friedrich Delitzsch and his pupils, Paul Haupt, Heinrich Zimmern, Paul Jensen, and Alfred Jeremias, assured its splendid development. The peak was attained by the publication of the three masterly works of Delitzsch himself, the *Assyrisches Wörterbuch* (1887), the *Assyrische Grammatik* (1889), and the *Assyrisches Handwörterbuch* (1896). Thereafter, workers who devoted their best efforts to the exploration of the immense field

---

Studies in the History of Writing in the Near East," *Haverford Symposium,* 111-135.

A selection of texts is given in Gressmann's work cited above, and in C. Jean, *Le Milieu biblique avant Jésus-Christ: I. Histoire et Civilisation; II. La Littérature; III. Les idées religieuses et morales* (Paris, 1922, 1923, 1936).

of Assyro-Babylonian literature and history were numerous in Germany, the United States, England, and France. The names of Fritz Hommel, Hermann V. Hilprecht, Ernst F. Weidner, Bruno Meissner, Benno Landsberger, Carl Bezold, Arthur Ungnad, Julius Lewy, Hans Bauer, Emil Forrer, Eckhard Unger, Hermann von Soden, Erich Ebeling, Anton Moortgat, Archibald Henry Sayce, Leonard William King, Harry Reginald Hall, Stephan Langdon, Daniel David Luckenbill, J. A. Knudtzon, Morris Jastrow, Albert Tobias Clay, Albert Ten Eyck Olmstead, Leroy Waterman, R. C. Thompson, Father Vincent Scheil, Edouard Dhorme, Louis Delaporte, Knut Tallqvist, François Thureau-Dangin, Henri de Genouillac, Charles F. Jean, Pierre Cruveilhier, Mariano San Nicolò, and Giuseppe Furlani figure in the advance. The *Chicago Assyrian Dictionary,* published under the direction of Arno Poebel, enables us to measure the progress achieved in the course of the last forty years.

The ancient Babylonians preserved the memory of the Sumerians, a people who preceded them in lower Mesopotamia and from whom they borrowed the best elements of their civilization. Their historical knowledge of this people seems to date back to 3200 B. C. The Sumerians themselves disappeared from the scene about the year 2000 B. C., at the time of the campaigns launched by Hammurabi and his Amorrhitic Semites against Babylon and the other cities of the lower Mesopotamian plain. In fact, after the year 2000, Sumerian seems to have become a dead language. It continued to be taught by the priests, however, down to the dawn of the Christian era, for it served a liturgical purpose, just as do Latin and Hebrew. Friedrich Delitzsch did the pioneer work also in Sumerian literature. In the course of the fateful year which ushered in the First World War (1914), he published his *Grundzüge der sumerischen Grammatik* and *Sumerisches Glossar*. Other grammars followed: Poebel's *Grundzüge der sumerischen Grammatik* in 1923; C. J. Gadd's *Sumerian Reading Book* in 1924; and Howardy's *Clavis Cuneorum* in 1933. Still more recently Father Anton Deimel of the Pontifical Biblical Institute, a distinguished scholar whose collaborators, Maurus Witzel, Nicolaus Schneider, and A. Pohl, do credit to the Institute, undertook the publication of a large Sumerian lexicon which was completed in 1934.

The popularity of cuneiform symbols throughout the Near East in ancient times is well known. Their use was not limited to the three principal languages of Mesopotamia, Sumerian, Accadian, and Assyrian, but they were also adopted farther east by Old Persian and Susian — to mention only two tongues. The trilingual inscription of Behistun-Persepolis, carved by command of Darius the Great and set forth in Accadian, Old Persian, and Susian, was lettered in cuneiform, and thus provided the key for the decipherment of this form of writing. In the west, cuneiform was adopted for the Hittite and the Phœnician of Ugarit-Ras Shamra, two languages which at present occupy the foreground of Oriental studies. Hittite documents, the collection of which was begun about 1877 by the Englishman Archibald Henry Sayce, are well on the way toward decipherment. Emil Forrer, Johann Friedrich, Albrecht Götze, Ferdinand Sommer, E. H. Sturtevant, and Bedrich Hrozny have expended a great amount of energy on the task. Since the work of P. Meriggi (1928) and as a result of the researches of Forrer, I. J. Gelb, H. T.

Bossert, and Hrozny, the Hittite texts in hieroglyphics and pictographs are also about to give up their secrets.[23]

The main linguistic interest of the Ras Shamra writings, already alluded to, lies in the fact that they furnish us with an alphabetic type of cuneiform for a language akin to Phœnician, Chanaanite, and Hebrew — a language indeed in which may be sought one of the archetypes of Chanaanite-Phœnician. Despite the numerous studies of the new documents which have appeared, we are just beginning to get a glimpse of the treasures of archæological, linguistic, and historical information about the Near East, and in particular about the land of Chanaan, which the 1500 B. C. library of Ras Shamra contains. We know that the Ugarit writings are reviving the problem of the origin of the alphabet which was raised by the Proto-Sinaitic inscriptions, found by Petrie in 1906 and partially deciphered by Gardiner in 1917. This literature will also shed new light on the literary forms of the Old Testament.

Space forbids consideration of the progress made in the history of the peoples who lived in the vicinity of the Fertile Crescent. Some of them have just begun to be rediscovered — Mitannians, Subarreans, Hurrites or Hurrians, Louites: unidentified nomads of the Syro-

23. On the deciphering of Hittite and the history of that people, read E. Dhorme, "Où en est le déchiffrement des hiéroglyphes hittites?", *Syria*, XIV (1933), 341-367; W. Couvreur, *De Hettitische H. Een Bijdrage tot de Studie van het Indo-europeesche vocalisme*, Bibliothèque du Muséon, V (Louvain, 1937); L. Delaporte, *Les Hittites* (Paris, La Renaissance du Livre, 1936); Götze, *Hethiter, Churriter und Assyrer* (Oslo, 1936; Harvard University Press, 1936); E. Forrer, "The Hittites in Palestine," *Quarterly Statement of the Palestine Exploration Fund* (1936), 190-203, and *Palestine Exploration Quarterly* (1937), 100-115. From these data Hooke (*Rec. Rev.*, 364) draws some questionable conclusions on the subject of the Hittites of the Bible.

Arabian desert and of Southern Arabia.[24] This last region, because of the supposed kinship of some of its traditions with those of the Bible and also because of the theory of the Arabian origin of the Semites, deserves special attention from exegetes who are also Orientalists. Nielsen, Rhodokanakis, and G. Ryckmans of Louvain have already achieved notable results in this field.[25]

In the presence of such material, as varied as it is abundant, there can be no surprise at the fact that the science of comparative Orientology developed only in recent years. An indispensable instrument for the philological and historical interpretation of ancient writings, it had been too long neglected, especially in view of the remarkable achievements of the comparative method during the last century in the field of Indo-European languages. Latterly, however, Orientalists have seemed anxious to make up for lost time. Furtwängler, Pottier, Andrae, Schäder, Moortgat, and Herzfeld have brilliantly inaugurated the study of comparative archæology. Comparative linguistics, tackled years ago by Brockelmann, a talented pioneer, has been revived by Landsberger, Bergsträsser,

---

24. Contenau, *La civilisation des Hittites et des Mitanniens* (Paris, 1934) ; Ungnad, *Subartu: Beiträge zur Kulturgeschichte und Völkerkunde Vorderasiens* (Berlin-Leipzig, 1936) ; Götze, *op. cit.* (cf. *ETL,* XIV [1937], 366-7) ; M. Berkooz, *The Nuzi Dialect of Akkadian: Orthography and Phonology* (Philadelphia, 1937) ; E. A. Speiser, "Notes on Hurrian Phonology," *JAOS,* LVIII (1938), 173-201, and "Ethnic Movements in the Near East in the Second Millenium B. C.," *Annual of the American Schools of Oriental Research,* XIII (1933), 13-54; Albright, *The Archaeology of Palestine and the Bible* (3rd ed., Philadelphia, 1935). On the Hurrians and the Bible, read Montgomery in *Rec. Rev.,* 3-4, and Hooke, *ibid.,* 360-1.

25. D. S. Margoliouth, *The Relations between Arabs and Israelites* (London, 1924) ; Montgomery, *Arabia and the Bible* (Philadelphia, 1934), and "The Present State of Arabian Studies," *Haverford Symposium.*

and Louis H. Gray.[26] Moreover, the history of comparative literature is coming into its own in the publications
of Jeremias, Schott, Pieper, and Grapow. Lastly, enterprising Orientalists in all the larger countries are publishing imposing syntheses. Jacques de Morgan may be cited
for Oriental prehistory; Erman, Sethe, Kees, Breasted,
Moret, and Wrezcinski for Egypt; Meissner, Jeremias, and
Olmstead for Assyro-Babylonia; Götze for Asia Minor;
Watzinger and Contenau for Palestine and Syria; and
Nielsen for Arabia. Two encyclopædias, the *Reallexikon
der Vorgeschichte* and the *Reallexikon der Assyriologie,*
will when completed render in the Oriental field the services which Daremberg-Saglio in France and Pauly-Wissowa
in Germany have rendered to classical studies.

A new world has arisen from the chantiers of the
ancient Near East since 1876, the year of the great
Wellhausen offensive. Is it surprising that this world has
reversed the picture of the history of Israel as the faithful
disciples of Wellhausen imagined it? What is left of the
theory that the Israelites were an isolated people, endowed
with unique intellectual and moral aptitudes which made
them the natural champions of monotheism in the pre-
Christian pagan world? Nothing, or practically nothing.[27]

---

26. L. H. Gray, *Introduction to Semitic Comparative Linguistics*
(New York, 1934); Zellig S. Harris, *Development of the Canaanite Dia-
lects: An Investigation in Linguistic History,* American Oriental Series,
XVI (New Haven, 1939).

27. See H. R. Hall, "Israel and the Surrounding Nations," *The
People and the Book,* 1-40; G. R. Driver, "The Modern Study of the
Hebrew Language," *ibid.,* 73-120; A. Jirku, *Altorientalischer Kommentar
zum Alten Testament* (Leipzig, 1923); A. Jeremias, *Das Alte Testament
im Lichte des Alten Orients* (4th ed., Leipzig, 1930); *Myth and Ritual:
Essays on the Myth and Ritual of the Hebrews in Relation to the Culture
Pattern of the Ancient East,* ed. Hooke (London, 1933); Meek, *Hebrew
Originˁ; The Labyrinth: Further Studies in the Relation between Myth*

Where do the Israelites belong in history? We may follow the standard long chronology and put the migration of Abraham at 2000 B. C. and the Exodus at 1450. Or we may adopt a more conservative reckoning with Abraham appearing either in 1800-1700 (era of the migration of the Hyksos and Hurrians) or in 1500 (date of the Habiri migration), and the Exodus taking place in 1225-1215 (reign of Merneptah). But no matter what chronological system is chosen, a comparison with other Oriental peoples — for instance, with the prehistoric races to whom we owe the civilizations of Badari, Al-Ubaid, Uruk, Djemdet Nasr, and Ghassul, as well as with the Egyptians, Sumerians, Babylonians, and Assyrians — shows that the earliest ancestors of Israel and the tribes which formed a confederation under Moses and Josue appear as latecomers on the historical scene.[28]

The myth of spiritual isolation, which was designed to explain without supernatural factors the unique progress Israel made in the realm of religious and moral ideas, vanishes also like a summer mist. If thought be given to the mingling of peoples and civilizations which took place in Palestine, and which makes that country comparable to the cauldron of Shakespeare's three witches, there can no longer be any question of it.[29]

---

and Ritual in the Ancient World, ed. Hooke (London, 1935) ; The Haverford Symposium; Record and Revelation.

28. On Biblical chronology, see Coppens, En marge de l'Histoire sainte, 27-47, and ETL, XIV (1937), 640-1; R. de Vaux, "La Palestine et la Transjordanie au IIᵉ millénaire et les origines israélites," ZAW, XV (1938), 225-238.

29. Historians and archæologists are agreeing more and more on the syncretic character of the Israelites and their civilization. See supra, note 27.

From the standpoint of race, it should be recalled that the Bible represents Abraham as coming from the district of Ur in Chaldea (Gen. xi, 31). It describes Jacob as an Aramean nomad (Deut. xxvi, 5). It

Finally, it is unscientific to extol the aptitudes and qualities of the people of Israel with, once again, the thinly veiled purpose of setting aside a supernatural explanation of Hebrew prophetism and monotheism. "Let us limit ourselves to remarking," writes P. Humbert, "that Israel was not richly endowed by the Muses: it never felt an imperious artistic vocation, the field of its imagination was quite narrow, and above all its taste was quite undeveloped. . . . Scientific interests appear not only to have been foreign to Israel but even to have become an object of its suspicion. [Finally] the word *nil* is not too strong to express Israel's unfitness for philosophy. It was a perfect vacuum."[30]

C. A third reaction against the tenets of the school of Wellhausen remains to be considered. It is the most important, since it concerns literary criticism itself. The multitude of different opinions on literary problems which the early disciples of Wellhausen had proclaimed settled once and for all, has caused a decline in the exuberant confi-

---

admits the partial fusion of the children of Israel with the Chanaanites and carries the ancestry of Israel back to Amorrhite and Hittite origins. It should be recalled also that the land of Chanaan was known to the Egyptians as the land of Hurru, and to the Assyrians as the land of Hattu. Specialists in ancient history are gradually giving these points more consideration. Montgomery and Hooke, while admitting that the terms "Habiru" and "Hyksos" are appellatives, fall back upon some sort of an identification of the Apiriu-Habiru-Ibrim, who swept down upon the land of Chanaan and Egypt in several waves of invasion, carrying along with them Hurrians, Semites, and other peoples. One of the first of these invading hordes came to be known in Egypt as the Hyksos. In connection with this, it is noted that the Egyptian language possesses two words for "chariot," one of which is said to be Hurrian and the other Semitic. See Hooke, *Rec. Rev.*, 362; also 2-3, 359, 363.

From the standpoint of culture, the same authors call attention to the syncretic character of the civilizations unearthed at Beth-Shan, Jericho, Tell ed-Duweir (Lachish), and Samaria. They insist that even the language of the Hebrews shows the marks of a very heterogeneous formation. See Thomas, "The Language of the Old Testament," *Rec. Rev.*, 374-402.

30. P. Humbert, "La Génie d'Israël," *RHPR,* VII (1927), 493-515.

dence of many critics in purely critico-literary methods. A new generation of exegetes has arisen. Under the leadership of Gressmann and Gunkel, they have spoken rather harsh words about their predecessors, calling them armchair philologists, bureaucrats of erudition, bookworms, Barnums of book-learning; accusing them of lack of vision and of disregarding the archæological and psychological discoveries, which alone make it possible to keep close to historic reality, to penetrate into the spirit of civilizations, and to grasp the sense of ancient literatures.

As a result of archæological discoveries, many authors no longer refuse to date a goodly number of Old Testament books earlier than classical Wellhausen criticism would have allowed. We know also that the beginning of writing, and even of alphabetic writing, goes back further than the time of Moses and that Palestine and Syria were the chosen lands for the first attempts at such writing. Let us recall in passing the Proto-Sinaitic texts, the inscription on the stele of Balua, the pseudo-hieroglyphic epigraphs of Byblos and Hama-Hamath, the alphabetic inscription of Akhîrâm, the very ancient inscriptions of Lachish, and the alphabetic texts of Ras Shamra. We can henceforth refer, as to passages meriting full confidence, to the once bitterly contested reports of Judges, v, 14 and viii, 14.[31]

The school of comparative history asserts that the classical Wellhausen system is incapable of reconstructing the history of Israelite literature on a basis of written

---

31. Judges v, 14: "and from Zebulun those who carry the staff of the scribe"; viii, 14: "so that he *wrote* down." Cf. *Rec. Rev.*, 8-9, 10-11, and J. Février, "La génèse de l'alphabet," *Revue des Cours et Conférences,* XL (1939), 704-732; Flight (cf. note 22).

documents alone. In order to do so, the followers of
Wellhausen are compelled to rely blindly on the manu-
script tradition of the Masoretes or of the Septuagint. On
the doubtful details of these textual traditions they must
then base all sorts of tenuous and daring arguments,
"ebenso geistreich wie kühn und ebenso kühn wie
geistreich" ("as witty as risky and as risky as witty") in
their efforts to dispute the authenticity, historicity, and
exact meaning of the inspired writings. Now that the
foundations for such arguments have been shown to be
patently unsound, it is clear how shallow the arguments
themselves must be. Countless are the vicissitudes which
the Sacred Text has undergone, and the editings and
revisions to which it has been subjected.[32] This fact, which
presents itself ever more clearly, is especially evident from
the recent discoveries of manuscripts and papyri reproducing fragments of the original text or of ancient versions. The author has in mind: the Nash papyrus, the
discovery of which goes back some years; the Hebrew
text of Ecclesiasticus found in the genizah of the ancient
synagogue of Cairo; several papyri or manuscripts linking
up with the Septuagint, viz., the Berlin fragments, the
Chester Beatty Biblical papyri, the John Rylands Library
Biblical papyri, the John H. Scheide papyri, and the Freer
Library Minor Prophets, to mention only the principal
acquisitions.[33] While these new witnesses to the Biblical

---

32. The bibliography of this subject has grown considerably in
recent years. See Coppens, *En marge de l'Histoire sainte,* 7-11, and "Pour
une nouvelle Version latine du Psautier," *ETL,* XV (1938), 5-33, especially footnotes 20 and 21; P. Kahle, "Der alttest. Bibeltext," *TR,* V
(1933), 227-238; G. Bertram: "Zur Septuaginta-Forschung: I. Textausga-
ben der Septuaginta," *ibid.,* III (1931), 283-296, "II. Das Textproblem
der Septuaginta," *ibid.,* V (1933), 173-186, "III. Das Problem der
Umschrifttexte," *ibid.,* X (1938), 69-80, 133-159.
33. Montgomery, *Rec. Rev.,* 26-7.

text were being studied, Paul Kahle of Bonn and A. Sperber of Cincinnati undertook in a scholarly work of vast erudition to get beyond the Masoretic Hebrew text by investigating the traces it still carries of more ancient punctuation and revision.[34] The unreliability of the basic text has been established, at any rate in the use of, and altenation in the Pentateuch of, the divine names, *Yahweh* and *Elohim*. This is an important observation, for it will be remembered that the alternate use of these names is one of the standard arguments on which the documentary theory has depended since the times of Witter, d'Astruc, Eichhorn, and Ilgen.[35] De Rossi (1780), J. D. Michaelis (1767), and J. Ph. Plüschke (1837) had long before expressed doubts on the trustworthiness of the Masoretic text in this regard. Since their day these doubts have been made the object of searching study, which tends to weaken the argument based on the text. This has been recognized by a succession of notable writers: A. Klostermann (1893),

34. E. Cardinal Tisserant, "Histoire et critique du Texte de l'Ancien Testament," *Initiation biblique* (Paris, 1938), 227-248. For a more elaborate study see Z. Frankel: *Vorstudien zu der Septuaginta* (Leipzig, 1841), and *Ueber den Einfluss der palästinischen Exegese auf die alexandrinische Hermeneutik* (Leipzig, 1851); Loisy, *Histoire du texte et des versions de la Bible: I. Histoire du texte hébreu de l'Ancien Testament* (Amiens, 1892); Kuenen, *Les Origines du Texte masorétique de l'Ancien Testament. Examen critique d'une récente hypothèse* (Paris, Leroux, 1875), trans. from the Dutch by A. Carrière; A. Geiger, *Urschrift und Uebersetzungen der Bibel in ihrer Abhängigkeit von der innern Entwicklung des Judentums* (1857; 2nd ed., Frankfort on the Main, 1928). See also note 32.

Even a hasty glance at some recent work, such as P. A. H. de Boer, *Research into the Text of I Samuel I-XVI: A Contribution to the Study of the Books of Samuel* (Amsterdam, 1938), reveals the enormous amount of labor involved in careful correction of the accepted text, at least if one tries to follow an objective method. See the present author's review of this work in *Chronique d'Ancien Testament*, 11-12.

35. U. Cassuto, *La Questione della Genesi* (Florence, 1934); C. Bernheimer, "La Questione della Genesi di Umberto Cassuto," *Rivista degli Studi Orientali*, XVI (1937), 307-336; Cassuto, "La mia Questione della Genesi," *ibid.*, 337-374.

J. Dahse (1903), Johann Lepsius (1903), H. Redpath
(1904), F. Hommel (1904), B. Eerdmans (1908), H. M.
Wiener (1910-1912), F. Baumgartel (1914), P. Metzger
1925), E. Sellin (1924), and F. M. T. Böhl (1930). The
same uncertainty prevails in regard to *Adonai,* another
divine name, found in both the Pentateuch and the prophetical writings.[36] Finally, we know how uncertain are
the references to Juda and to Israel, and also how vague
is the meaning of the latter term in the utterances of Old
Testament prophets.[37]

Not only the wording but also the original meaning
of the texts eluded the critics. No matter how obvious and
clear that meaning may seem, it is much more difficult to
grasp than the commentators of the last half-century believed. They, indeed, lived in an atmosphere of philological complacency which was due no doubt to the contemporary progress in Oriental linguistics, and were easily
satisfied. But, to say the least, the error of the Wellhausen
school in trying to read the ancient texts without sufficient
preparation, was a serious one. It attempted to discuss,
analyze, and dissect in the light of literary precepts borrowed solely from manuals of Greco-Roman and modern
literature. It presumed to judge the value and the composition of the Sacred Books according to its own modern
norms and æsthetic taste. Certain writers of the school,
like pedantic schoolmasters enamored of grammar, logical

36. W. von Baudissin, *Kyrios als Gottesname und seine Stelle in
der Religionsgeschichte,* ed. Eissfeldt (Giessen, 1926-1929), 4 vols.; L.
Cerfaux, "Le nom divin 'Kyrios' dans la Bible grècque," *Revue des sciences philosophiques et théologiques,* XX (1931), 25-51; "Adonai et
Kyrios," *ibid.,* 417-452.

37. For an example of the hypotheses developed on revision of the
text, see R. E. Wolfe, "The Editing of the Book of the Twelve," *ZAW,*
XII (1935), 90-129. On the attestation of Juda and Israel, see L. Rost,
Israel bei den Propheten, BWANT, 4th ser., fasc. 19 (Stuttgart, 1937).

analysis, and literary precept, refused any quarter to the inspired writers for the slightest literary imperfection or peccadillo. They slashed to the marrow, cut and recut the text, transposed, suppressed, added to, and substituted for, the received wording. In short, they arbitrarily reconstructed the text of the Sacred Books whenever it had the bad grace to be not to their liking.

Now that the passage of time enables us to view the work of the Wellhausen school in better perspective, these methods seem all but inconceivable. And yet they were employed almost constantly in the commentaries of the Buddes, the Duhms, the Martis, and the Wellhausens. It is hard to explain how they could have originated and established themselves. In the view of the writer the reason why the Wellhausen critics attributed their own pet ideas to ancient authors is chiefly that they forgot the counsel of the *Following of Christ:* "Omnis scriptura eo spiritu debet legi quo scripta est."

The comparative study of literatures, the history of religions, and form criticism have also rendered very great services to the cause of Biblical exegesis. They have taught us to delve anew into the spirit of the ancient texts: first, by comparative study of the ancient Eastern literatures, and secondly by systematic study of the various literary types in the literature of Israel itself, even in the most minute examples. The concomitant use of these methods alone makes it possible for us to reconstruct the canons of ancient literature, both for the total deposit and for individual authors. Certain oddities or imperfections of Israelite style, which in days gone by gave the cue for arbitrary corrections of text or for fantastic arguments against authenticity, are now definitely explained as genu-

ine standard constructions of ancient Oriental style.[38] Like
every other literature, that of the ancient East possesses
special characteristics of its own that confuse the uniniti-
ate. We are now beginning to understand clearly that the
ancient Orientals affected repetitions, echoing phrases,
long speeches, and an inflated rhetoric. We have learned
the principles of their imagery and poetry. We even know
the conventions and peculiarities of their various styles:
prophetic, apocalyptic, sapiential, and devotional. The best
work, at present, from the standpoint of the history of
literary forms is unquestionably that of Professor Hempel,
published in the Berlin series, *Handbuch der Literaturwis-
senschaft*.[39] It marks the triumph of the new outlook.
In short, what Joseph Bédier and Victor Bérard achieved
for some of the ancient epics, the Gunkel-Gressmann-
Hempel school has successfully accomplished in the Biblical sphere.[40]

---

38. See an attempt to take the new conclusions into account as
early as 1923 in Baumgartner, "Ein Kapitel vom hebräischen Erzählungs-
stil," *Gunkel-Festschrift* (1923), 152 ff.

39. Prof. W. A. Irwin of the University of Chicago takes me to
task for including J. Hempel among the followers of the new methods
(*Journal of Religion*, XIX [1939], 384). I am aware that the German
scholar remains faithful to what he himself calls three bastions of Wellhausen criticism: the dating of Deuteronomy as the law of Josias (621),
the description of Ezechiel xl-xlviii as the Exilic anticipation of the
Priestly Code, and the interpretation of the Priestly Code within the
historical setting of Nehemias viii-x. All this, however, does not prevent
the general character, inspiration, and tendencies of the entire work from
being quite other than those of the Wellhausen type.

40. See Coppens, *En marge de l'Histoire sainte*, 21-23, and espe-
cially Hempel, *Althebräische Literatur u. ihr hellenistisch-jüdisches
Nachleben*. Many useful points may also be found in the following
studies: Andreas Heusler, *Nibelungensage und Nibelungenlied* (1920);
H. M. Chadwick-N. K. Chadwick, *The Growth of Literature: I. The
Ancient Literatures of Europe* (Cambridge, 1932); F. C. Grant, "Form
Criticism Farther Afield," *Anglican Theological Review*, XIX (1937),
181-6; H. G. Güterbock, "Die historische Tradition und ihre literarische
Gestaltung bei Babyloniern und Hethitern bis 1200," *Zeitschrift für
Assyriologie* XLIV (1938), 45-149; Wolfgang Schadewalt, "Homer und

Lastly, if the classical Wellhausen method of criticism is incapable — and we have seen that it is — of solving with its own instruments the problems of the interpretation, integrity, and authenticity of ancient books, then it should also forego any attempt to establish the chronology, whether relative or absolute, of Israelite literature. At one time, however, it did make this attempt, recommending for the task two scales of comparison: its own evolutional chart of Israelite religion, and *Zeitgeschichte,* that is to say, the systematic employment of alleged Biblical allusions to key events of profane history. Since definite historical allusions were found not to be very numerous, the first of these two scales was the more frequently utilized.

Once again the school of comparative history has demonstrated the inadequacy of these two criteria and of the hypotheses to which they lent support. There is nothing more artificial, as we have already seen, than the evolutional chart of the religion of Israel drawn up by the classical school of Wellhausen. Moreover, the historical data are so meager that they do not justify the elaboration of any system of chronology having even the slightest claim to completeness.

The new school, not satisfied with doing work of a negative character, also evolved a fresh, more objective, and yet extremely delicate instrument of chronological research. Relying on the few securely dated Biblical writings, the dated documents of other Oriental literatures, and also the "situation in life" (*Sitz im Leben*) of im-

die Homerische Frage," *Die Antike* (1938), 1-29; Jérome Tharaud, "Discours de réception à l'Académie française sur l'oeuvre de Joseph Bédier," *Le Temps,* January 19, 1940.

portant literary productions, it tried to reconstruct the internal development of the several literary forms represented in the Bible. With the assistance of the chronologico-literary sliding scale thus established, it then passed judgment, warily it is true, on the relative and absolute dates of composition of the principal books of the various groups. The new school undoubtedly knows that these scales of comparison also are defective. Nothing proves, for example, that literary forms evolve according to regular progression. There might have been, conceivably, a step forward, then a decline, then an unexpected renascence. This might happen spontaneously, or it might be brought about by borrowing, restoration, or the creative powers of gifted personalities. Such cases must, however, have been exceptional. For ordinary purposes the sliding scale will prove useful, provided its employment is regulated by application of all the other apparatus, including the few allusions to the key events of profane history which we have at our disposal.[41]

The new school launches a third fundamental indictment against the critics. Inadequate for the reconstruction of the literary history of Israel, the classical Wellhausen system has shown itself still more incapable of reconstructing on the basis of written documents alone the political and religious history of the Hebrews.

Who in our day would dream of reviving the daring axiom of the first followers of Wellhausen, "Quod non est in actis non est in re"? As has been shown above, archæological findings, even in Palestine, have brought to light a world of whose very existence the first critics had no

---

41. Hempel, *op. cit.*, 19-101.

suspicion. It is now definitely established that Biblical documentation for whole periods is fragmentary. Consequently, the silences of the Sacred Books must be interpreted with the greatest circumspection. On the other hand, too, a certain amount of Scriptural assertion once called into question by critics has found sensational confirmation. Not a report comes from the excavators which does not provide a remarkable verification of Biblical traditions on some special point or other.

Even where the Sacred Texts have much to say about a given period, the Wellhausen system proves inadequate for understanding them completely. The classical theory of that system bases the history of Israel on the solution of problems in literary criticism. Now, as we have just seen, these solutions are frequently unreliable even when not tainted by prejudice. Furthermore, even assuming the Wellhausen positions to be sufficiently substantiated in other respects, the school of comparative history attacks them on two other scores. The system, it charges, has not taken into consideration the oral prehistory of the written documents;[42] neither has it tried to explain them on a

---

42. The value of oral tradition is likewise admitted for the writings of the New Testament. The researches and conclusions of Père M. Jousse in this field — Le style orale et mnémotechnique chez les verbo-moteurs: Études de Psychologie linguistique (Paris, 1925) — are well known. They must be used cautiously but they are not without their value. The problem of oral tradition affects several great literary productions of antiquity, especially the Zend-Avesta. We, who are children of the paper age, and great bookworms besides, can hardly appreciate the strength of memory that the primitives and ancients possessed.

On the history of Israel, see Cook, "L'arrière-plan historique de l'Ancien Testament," RHPR, IX (1929), 295-318; Galling, "Geschichte Israels," TR, II (1930), 94-128; Cook, "Salient Problems in Old Testament History," JBL, LI (1932), 273-299; Albright, "The History of Palestine and Syria," Jewish Quarterly Review, XXIV (1934), 363-376; Causse, Du groupe ethnique à la communauté religieuse (Paris, Alcan, 1937).

more objective basis in the light of the religious and literary history of the ancient East, and of a better psychological understanding of the ancient peoples, even though contemporary research in religious phenomenology provides us with the means of doing so. Hempel's work on the literary history of Israel has been matched in psychological appreciation of the primitive mentality by J. Pedersen in his book, *Israel: Its Life and Cuture* (Oxford, 1926), and in a more general way by G. Van der Leeuw in *Phänomenologie der Religion* (Tübingen, 1933) and *De Primitieve Mensch en de Religie* (Groningen, 1937).

II. The Principal New Literary Results

Up to this point I have outlined the leading anti-Wellhausen reactions whose far-reaching and steadily-increasing, if somewhat subterranean, activity has compromised the prestige of the critical school. But more can be done than merely to set forth these general considerations, whatever be their scope and the effects which they have had and will continue to have on the development of Biblical studies. Indeed, nothing will help us more to understand the revolution that has taken place than an exposition of how the problems and the solutions have changed. We shall once again, all too rapidly it must be admitted, skim over the entire field of Biblical literature, considering the various inspired books according to the principal categories.[43]

In the first chapter I intimated that the struggles which the sapiential literature occasioned were relatively

---

43. For a good analytical and critical retrospective bibliography, see Pfeiffer, "The History, Religion, and Literature of Israel: Research in the Old Testament, 1914-1925," *HThR*, XXVII (1934), 241-325.

few.[44] Because the conservative wing of exegetes adopted the critical positions, the contest was never bitter. The most significant event was the discovery and comparative study of literary works of other Oriental literatures. For some time, attention centered about a Babylonian document in which a parallel was thought to have been found either to the Book of Job or to Ecclesiastes,[45] since each was in turn mentioned. But this set-piece served up on the table of comparative literature has proved to be a collection of Egyptian sayings known as the *Wisdom of Amen-em-Apet*. Allowances must be made, of course, for the initial enthusiasm which attended the translation and

---

44. Baumgartner, "Die israelitische Weisheitsliteratur," *TR*, V (1933), 259-288; Galling, "Stand und Aufgabe der Kohelet-Forschung," *ibid.*, VI (1934), 355-373; C. Kuhl, "Das Hohelied und seine Deutung," *ibid.*, IX (1937), 137-167; Hilaire Duesberg, *Les Scribes inspirés: I. Le Livre des Proverbes* (Paris, 1938); A. Vaccari, "Il Cantico dei Cantici nelle recenti pubblicazioni," *Bi*, IX (1928), 443-457; H. H. Rowley, "The Interpretation of the Song of Songs," *JTS*, XXXVIII (1937), 337-363; Pfeiffer, "Wisdom and Vision," *ZAW*, XI (1934), 93-101; *The Song of Songs: A Symposium*, by M. L. Margolis, J. A. Montgomery, W. W. Hyde, F. Edgerton, T. J. Meek, and W. H. Schoff (Philadelphia, 1924). Among the latest important publications in English may be noted: Harry Ranston, *The Old Testament Wisdom Books and Their Teaching* (London, 1930); D. B. Macdonald, *The Hebrew Philosophical Genius As Manifested in the Wisdom Literature: A Vindication* (Princeton, 1936); O. S. Rankin, *Israel's Wisdom Literature: Its Bearing on Theology and the History of Religion* (Edinburgh, 1936). Cf. Barton, "The Present State of Old Testament Studies," *Haverford Symposium*, 69-72.

45. E. Ebeling, *Ein babylonischer Qohelet*, Berliner Beiträge zur Keilschriftforschung, I (Berlin, 1922); P. Dhorme, "Ecclésiaste ou Job?" *RB*, XXXII (1923), 5-27; Lods, "Recherches récentes sur le Livre de Job," *RHPR*, XIV (1934), 501-533.

The hypothesis that Ecclesiastes is a natural outgrowth of Semitic viewpoints to which certain Babylonian texts furnish a parallel, was proposed thirty years ago by G. A. Barton. This position was challenged in 1925 by the New Zealand scholar, Harry Ranston. He contended that Ecclesiastes was profoundly influenced by Greek thought, particularly that of Theognis. See his *Ecclesiastes and the Early Greek Wisdom Literature* (London, 1925). Morris Jastrow follows a middle course: *A Gentle Cynic: Being the Book of Ecclesiastes* (Philadelphia, 1919).

study of this collection. If they do nothing else, the proverbs of the Egyptian sage, some of which closely resemble those of the Biblical tradition, prove that sapiential literature in the East is of very ancient vintage.[46] The reputation of Solomon as the Israelite sage par excellence has accordingly gained in historical likelihood. More than that — there is no longer any objection to pushing back the traditions of the Hebrew sages to a remote epoch and even to assigning them a certain measure of influence in the perfecting of Hebrew monotheism. Even the historicity of prophetical literature finds neat confirmation in the new outlook. Long before the Exile, it numbered sages along with prophets and priests.[47]

Was there in addition to these three classes of the nation's spiritual leaders a fourth group, comprised of the cantors, religious poets of devotional circles, and perhaps cult prophets, as they have been called? The question has been vigorously but fruitlessly debated. At any rate, devotional (*piétiste*) literature, particularly as found in the Psalms, appears much more ancient than Wellhausen and his school would admit. The great expert in this field was the talented Hermann Gunkel. The theory of literary forms which he applied to the Psalter is in reality very simple and in certain respects as old as exegesis of the Psalms. But as in the case of Christopher Columbus and the egg, he had to think it out and turn it to advantage. Promised in numerous articles, and applied in his great

---

46. P. Humbert, *Recherches sur les sources égyptiennes de la littérature sapientiale d'Israël* (Neuchâtel, 1929); E. A. Wallis Budge, *The Teaching of Amen-em-Apet, son of Kanecht* (London, 1924).

47. L. Borlée, *Hakam et Hokmah dans la littérature hébraïque jusqu'à Esdras* (mimeographed dissertation submitted to the Theological Faculty of Louvain, 1929). See especially, Jeremias xviii, 18 and Ezechiel vii, 26.

commentary of 1926, his theory found its classic expression in a posthumous work which remains to the present the best literary introduction to the study of the Psalter.[48]

Gunkel, however, did more than supply us with a few good works: he succeeded in spreading his influence abroad by the formation of eminent pupils. One of these, Sigmund Mowinckel, Gunkel's brilliant second, yields to his master neither in originality of thought nor in prolific literary activity. It would be impossible to describe here even the main points of the work of this most influential of Norwegian exegetes. Many of his conclusions, in the present author's opinion, leave something to be desired. But a great, and this the better, part of his work — not merely a few conclusions — withstands testing. The amount of patiently assembled documentation is imposing and vast. The spirit of his work and his viewpoint are in the main new: along the lines which they indicate, all future study of the Psalter will have to be conducted. Lastly, a few general theses are particularly strong.[49] These may be summed up as follows: 1) The Psalter is an anthology of cult prayers,[50] and consequently it

---

48. Gunkel, *Einleitung in die Psalmen: Die Gattungen der religiösen Lyrik Israels*, ed. J. Begrich (1928-1933). See also *The Psalmists: Essays on Their Religious Experience and Teaching, Their Social Background, and Their Place in the Development of Hebrew Psalmody*, ed. David C. Simpson (Oxford, 1926) ; M. Haller, "Ein Jahrzehnt Psalmforschung," *TR*, I (1928), 377-402; Begrich; "Zur Hebräischen Metrik," *ibid.*, IV (1932), 67-89; Oesterley, *A Fresh Approach to the Psalms* (London, 1937).

49. Mowinckel, *Psalmenstudien: I. Awän und die individuellen Klagepsalmen; II. Das Thronbesteigungsfest Jahwäs und der Ursprung der Eschatologie; III. Kultprophetie und prophetische Psalmen; IV. Die technischen Termini in dem Psalmenüberschriften; V. Segen und Fluch in Israels Kult und Psalmendichtung; VI. Die Psalmendichter* (Oslo, 19211924).

50. See G. Quell, *Das kultische Problem der Psalmen, BWAT*, 2nd ser., fasc. 11 (Stuttgart, 1926).

would be a definite mistake to interpret it as a collection of meditations and prayers primarily intended for private devotions; 2) Its cult aspect derives from the liturgy of the pre-Exilic Temple and sanctuaries of Yahweh and not from that of the Second Temple; 3) The cult and pre-Exilic character can be established critically for at least three groups — the royal Psalms, the Psalms of the *anawim* (the poor, sick, and oppressed), and the Psalms of the royal enthronement of Yahweh.[51]

Revolutionary though the above conclusions may be, in many respects those concerned with the prophetical literature appear even more striking. They stem from two lines of research: the first grew out of work on the history of ancient Oriental literature and harks back to Gunkel and his colleague Gressmann;[52] the second arose from the psychological interpretation of the prophets as inaugurated by the monograph of Gustav Hölscher, published in 1914.[53] It is no exaggeration to say that in no other field did the classical Wellhausen theses have to submit to such violent and radical revision. The celebrated antithetical division into pre-Exilic and post-Exilic prophets, introduced by Duhm and Wellhausen, no longer exists. Objections against the authenticity of eschatological prophecies

51. For a good orientation see the works cited in note 48, to which may be added: I. Loeb, *La littérature des Pauvres dans la Bible* (Paris, 1892); Causse, *Les "Pauvres" d'Israël: Prophètes, psalmistes, messianistes* (Paris, Alcan, 1922), and *Les plus vieux chants de la Bible* (Paris, Alcan, 1926); Harris Birkeland, *Ani und Anaw in den Psalmen* (Oslo, 1933), and *Die Feinde des Individuums in der israelitischen Psalmenliteratur* (Oslo, 1933); R. G. Castellino, *Le Lamentazioni individuali e gli inni in Babilonia e in Israele: Raffrontati riguardo alla forma e al contenuto* (Milan, 1939).

52. Gressmann: *Der Ursprung der israelitisch-jüdischen Eschatologie,* Forschungen zur Religion und Literatur des Alten und Neuen Testaments, fasc. 6 (Göttingen, 1905), and *Der Messias* (Göttingen, 1929).

53. Hölscher, *Die Propheten: Untersuchungen zur Religionsgeschichte Israels* (Leipzig, 1914).

and Messianic prophecies of better times, if they have not been utterly dissipated, have at least been very much weakened. Furthermore, a prophetical exegesis which is a thing of light and shadow has developed, and to the writer's way of thinking it finds its vindication in the monograph of Johann Lindblom, another eminent representative of Scriptural science in Nordic lands.[54]

From the standpoint of literary analysis, moreover, quite a strong opposition is growing up against the tendency to parcel out the prophetical writings into minute fragments devoid of any connection, and to interpret the least lack of coherence or the slightest variation from literary form as an indication of spuriousness. It is now held that quite appreciable incoherence and heterogeneity of matter are perfectly compatible with prophetical literature, provided allowance is made for its mystical aspect (J. Lindblom) or its liturgical character (H. Gunkel, P. Humbert), and provided, too, that a more important rôle is assigned to oral tradition in the preservation of prophetical writings (H. Birkeland).[55] Even the writers who continue to break up the prophetical books into several component parts show more moderation and reserve than

---

54. J. Lindblom, "Die Literarische Gattung der Prophetischen Literatur," *Uppsala Universitets Arsskrift, 1924: Teologi I* (Uppsala, 1924); "Hosea literarkritisch untersucht," *Acta Academiae Aboensis Humaniora,* V, 2 (Abo, 1928); "Micha literarisch untersucht," *ibid.,* VI, 2 (Abo, 1929).

On the prophetical literature as a whole, see Ed. Tobac-J. Coppens, *Les prophètes d'Israël: I. Le prophétisme en Israël* (2nd ed., Malines, 1932); T. H. Robinson, "Neuere Propheten-Forschung," *TR,* III (1931), 75-103; L. Köhler, "Amos-Forschungen von 1917 bis 1932," *ibid.,* IV (1932), 195-213; Kuhl, "Zur Geschichte der Hesekiel-Forschung," *ibid.,* V (1933), 92-118.

55. See *Rec. Rev.,* 93-4, and Birkeland, *Zum hebräischen Traditionswesen: Die Komposition der Prophetischen Bücher des Alten Testaments* (Oslo, 1938). In regard to this work, see the present author's *Chronique d'Ancien Testament,* 20.

formerly. T. H. Robinson's classification of prophetical traditions into elements B, C, and A, i. e., autobiographical elements written in the first person, biographical elements written in the third person, and collections of oracles, is an example in point.[56]

The historical literature of the ancient Hebrews has not profited to the same extent from the new hermeneutics. A glance at the commentaries of Gunkel and Gressmann on Genesis and the oldest historical writings of the Hebrews shows that critical opinion leans toward modification on two points: 1) The Yahwist and Elohist documents would be less the work of two authors than of two literary schools, and consequently their integrity would be compromised by reason of successive additions, alterations, and recensions which they had to undergo; 2) If this be the case, to establish their date of composition is far less important than to determine their oral and historical beginnings, their "situation in life" — a standpoint which allows for regression to a date much more remote than that on which the school of Wellhausen fixed.[57]

---

56. On the A elements (oracles), B elements (autobiographical accounts), and C elements (biographical accounts), see Mowinckel, *Zur Komposition des Buches Jeremias* (1914), and Robinson, *loc. cit.*

57. Gunkel, *Die Sagen der Genesis* (1901) and *Die Urgeschichte und die Patriarchen*, in Die Schriften des Alten Testaments ser. (2nd ed., Göttingen, 1921); Gressmann, *Die Anfänge Israëls, ibid.* (Göttingen, 1910; 2nd ed., 1922) and *Die älteste Geschichtsschreibung und Prophetie Israels, ibid.* (2nd ed., Göttingen, 1921); Lods, "Le rôle de la tradition orale dans la formation des récits de l'Ancien Testament," *Revue de l'Histoire des Religions,* LXXXVIII (1923), 51-64; Humbert, "Die neuere Genesis-Forschung," *TR,* VI (1934), 147-160, 207-228.

It is very interesting to note the conclusions recently reached by von Rad, a German critic who still favors the Wellhausen position in other respects. It is impossible to resist reproducing some of his conclusions, expressed in *Das formgeschichtliche Problem des Hexateuchs:*

1) "The Hexateuch in its present form is the work of redactors who felt themselves obliged to respect the individuality of each source-

Literary affinity between the Hexateuch and the Books of Judges, Samuel, and Kings is in general claimed with far less assurance. Certain writers are even venturing to suggest in explanation of their origin the existence of sources or documents peculiar to them. Such is the proposal of Leonard Rost, *Die Ueberlieferung von der Thronnachfolge David* (Stuttgart, 1926), and Harold M. Wiener, *The Composition of Judges II, 11 to I Kings, II, 46* (Leipzig, 1929).

It remains to say a word about the books of the Law, or more exactly, the various documents and codes of law

---

document in the expression of its religious testimony. . . . Many ages and men, many traditions and theologians, contributed to this gigantic work. Consequently, if one wishes to reach a true understanding of it, he cannot skim over it lightly: he must read it with an appreciation for its vast background" (72).

2) "The form of the Hexateuch was already definitely fixed upon by the Yahwist. The Elohist and the Priestly Code introduce no further change in this regard: they are merely aspects of that powerful Yahwistic conception although obviously of a greater theological individuality" (69).

3) "The Elohist's faithful adherence to tradition has always been stressed as one of his characteristics. . . . He writes more in the popular vein and consequently his way of presentation has always been considered the more ancient even though he appears in writing later than the Yahwist" (69).

4) "The Priestly Code works for the legitimation of religious ceremonial . . . in P the entire deposit of tradition, down to its details, is thus restored to the domain of the religious. In P, however, there is an entirely different sort of priestly-sacred thought than was the case in the old cult-traditions before they were taken over by the Yahwist [who laicized the ancient religious traditions]. The desire for legitimizing the sacred was thus not spent in safeguarding a mere custom, as was the case in the old cult-traditions. On the contrary, P sketches a whole course of history (from the creation of the world down to the text of the Covenant at Silo), in which God's saving dispensation was unmistakably revealed" (71).

5) "Taking the Yahwist as a norm, we can, in a certain sense, say that both E and P even incline toward a return to old ideas. In the Priestly Code an unmistakable restoration tendency is uppermost. This attitude is closely connected with the notion that the code originated in the reconstruction period of Josia and Ezra" (71-2).

6) "Deuteronomy appears to be a veritable baroque accumulation of cult materials, which however all reflect the same religious process, and what is more, represent the end of a decidedly long process of crystallization. The unity of structure is great . . . "(30).

which critical writers contended were to be found in the Pentateuch. It is, let it be noted at once, the field in which the comparative historical method and form criticism have made their influence felt last of all.

Among the authors who have attempted to demolish, or at least to dispute, the documentary theory, there is space only to mention J. Dahse, J. C. Aalders, M. Kegel, P. Metzger, W. Möller, J. Horovitz, B. Jacob, and U. Cassuto. Their observations concern only special aspects of the problem, or individual books, and they do not aim at replacing the Graf-Wellhausen hypothesis by another more complete and better substantiated. Before mentioning the studies undertaken from the standpoint of form criticism, however, the author desires to stress the researches of August Klostermann, Barend Dirk Eerdmans, Wilhelm Rudolph, Paul Volz, Harold M. Wiener, and Max Löhr.[58]

As early as 1904, H. L. Strack, well-known as a Hebrew scholar, while openly admitting that the great majority of critics in all lands had been won over to the Graf-Wellhausen theory, formulated certain reservations in the article "Pentateuch" in the *Realencyclopädie für protestantische Theologie und Kirche* (third edition).

---

58. Klostermann, *Der Pentateuch. Beiträge zu seinem Verständnis und seiner Entstehungsgeschichte,* I and II (Leipzig, 1893-1907) ; Eerdmans, *Alttestamentliche Studien: I. Die Komposition der Genesis; II. Die Vorgeschichte Israels; III. Das Buch Exodus; IV. Das Buch Leviticus* (Giessen, 1908, 1909, 1910, 1912) ; P. Volz-W. Rudolph, *Der Elohist als Erzähler ein Irrweg der Pentateuchkritik? An der Genesis erläutert* (Giessen, 1933) ; Rudolph, "Der Elohist von Exodus bis Josua," *BZAW,* 68 (Giessen, 1938) ; M. Löhr, *Der Priestercodex in Deuteronomium* (Berlin, 1925) ; H. M. Wiener: *Pentateuchal Studies* (London, 1912), *Essays in Pentateuchal Criticism* (London, 1910), *The Origin of the Pentateuch* (London, 1910). On the documentary theory and Genesis, we cannot omit to refer to Cassuto's work (see *supra,* note 35) and the commentary of B. Jacob, *Das erste Buch der Tora: Genesis übersetzt und erklärt* (Berlin, 1934). Cf. Coppens, *En marge de l'Histoire sainte,* 53-5.

He recalled the restrictions already proposed by August Dillmann in *Kommentar zu Nu-Dt-Jos* (Leipzig, 1886) as well as the objections of August Klostermann. Strack's reservations are worth recording: 1) No doubt Deuteronomy seems to be the code of Josias, but everything favors the belief that it is much more ancient than the reform undertaken by this king; 2) If the compilation of the Priestly Code is post-Exilic, then the Minor Law of Holiness (Leviticus xvii-xxvi was so called by Klostermann) is prior to Ezechiel, and other sacerdotal legislation is very probably ancient — at all events, prior to the Exile; 3) The definitive composition of the Hexateuch consisted in the incorporation of D into J E P and not, vice versa, of P into J E D, as Graf's theory would have it.

The articles of August Klostermann, published in various reviews and later collected in two volumes, are even more important than Strack's writings on the subject. After all, Strack merely repeated in a modified form the critical observations of August Dillmann to which we have referred.[59] Yet the original form of Klostermann's studies precludes any unity. He should have taken the trouble of rewriting them in order to eliminate lengthiness and digressions and make them a unified whole. Some difficulty is felt today in trying to grasp his system. It does not seem to have been fully worked out. He gives a rough sketch rather than a detailed plan of the solution he proposes. If the author has properly understood it, his system is a simplified documentary hypothesis, almost a theory of

---

59. Dillmann proposed the following dates: E ($\pm$800-750), H and Q ($\pm$800), J ($\pm$750), D ($\pm$622), Q+E+J ($\pm$600), Q E J +D (587-537), Q E J D+H+other sacerdotal *toroth* (before 444), the promulgation of Q E J D H by Esdras (444). In this system, the symbol Q represents the *Quattuor foederum Liber,* that is, the narrative sections of P and the laws relating thereto.

complements. He supposes that the Hexateuch is made up of two basic documents — the first, an ancient Pentateuch comprising Genesis, Exodus, Leviticus, Numbers and Josue and antedating King Josias; the second, Deuteronomy, a compilation of instructions in the Law, presumably committed to writing between the time of Samuel and Saul and that of David and Solomon, and found in the Temple during the reign of the Judean monarch mentioned above. Furthermore, as a basis for the ancient Pentateuch several documents must be distinguished: a collection of statistical data, compilations of narratives and various legal codes, in addition to a series of editings which concentrated on harmonizing and adapting the sources. The earlier editions produced a piecing together of the documents rather than a real recasting. This process would explain the ease with which some pericopes, even after being juxtaposed, wandered through the Hexateuch, and likewise the facility with which others were suppressed or new ones were added. Klostermann concluded that the definitive edition of the ancient Pentateuch very probably goes back to the years following the dedication of the Temple of Jerusalem. This deduction was based on the chronological system of the editors, which apparently hinges on the twentieth year of Solomon, the year of the dedication of the royal sanctuary of Yahweh. For the sources of the Hexateuch, the author studied principally the sacerdotal passages and the Book of the Covenant. For these he goes back to the Mosaic era, postulating a radical recasting of the Book of the Covenant and asserting that the sacerdotal traditions were definitely fixed by the written word for the most part during the reigns of David and Solomon. Klostermann's critical examination of the Book of the Covenant is one of the gems of his work and prepares the way for the discussions of Eerdmans on the same subject.

The work of August Klostermann leads us almost directly to the great critical achievements of Eerdmans, although the latter cites the productions of his predecessor comparatively infrequently. Eerdmans agrees with him, however, in several points of method, in several conclusions, and in a general anti-Wellhausen attitude. In other respects he decisively parts company with his German colleague. Instead of constructing, as Klostermann did, a vast system in which the panoramic overbalances the analytic, the Dutch professor dogs the footsteps of the critics and proves chapter by chapter and verse by verse the improbability of their positions. Then, using the very tools of his opponents, he substitutes for their views a theory of his own, or better, a set of new hypotheses. Unfortunately, he has not had the time to develop them completely, for in mid-career he became engaged in other pursuits, especially in politics — a rather exceptional case among Old Testament exegetes.

Let it be noted here and now that the question of the Pentateuch resolves itself, for Eerdmans, into at least three distinct problems dealing respectively with Genesis, Exodus and Leviticus, and Deuteronomy. Numbers he scarcely touched. He explains the origin of Genesis by a theory of complements, making the Book of *Toledoth* (Generations) the *Grundschrift* of the work (I, 83-88). For Exodus and Leviticus he revives the hypothesis of fragments. He believes, in fact, that originally the Israelite laws were not incorporated with the narratives (III, 146). Eerdmans concludes that nothing stands in the way of assigning the substance of the Book of the Covenant to the era of Moses. The laws collected in our Leviticus reflect the usages and customs of the Temple of Jerusalem. Their codification and promulgation under their present form trace back, except for post-Exilic amplifications, to King Ezechias. Lastly, Deuteronomy was the legal code promulgated in 621 B. C. under the Judean King Josias. Eerdmans adopts in good part the Riehm-Wellhausen critical solution to explain its literary origin. In each of these codes, and particularly in Leviticus, account should be taken of later additions and modifications, especially those introduced by the leaders of the new Jewish community after the Babylonian Exile.

The third great anti-Wellhausen critique was formulated in recent publications, which are partly the result of close collaboration, by two excellent German exegetes, neither of whom is in the least suspect of traditionalism: P. Volz and W. Rudolph. Their work does not treat of the laws but bears almost entirely on the narrative sections of the Hexateuch. They too favor, if not a theory of complements, at least a radical simplification of the documentary theory.

Volz admits only one narrator in Genesis, the Yahwist. Whatever so-called Elohistic or sacerdotal elements cannot be linked with the Yahwist document must be credited to glossarists, interpolators, commentators, editors, or compilers of the Israelite epic and laws. Löhr previously expressed the same idea in regard to the Priestly Code.

Rudolph likewise suppressed the Elohist narrator. He was at first doubtful about the priestly narrator, at least as far as Genesis was concerned. Later, the study of the other books of the Hexateuch so convinced him of the presence of a history written by a priest that he believed the conclusions of Volz in regard to Genesis would have to be revised on this particular point. In a word, the narrative sections of the Hexateuch would have to be divided between P and J. Of these two documents, the Yahwist is by far the more important: its author seems to have been as much a collector of traditions as an independent and original writer. Besides, not a few of his pericopes must have been transposed and additions must have been inserted into his work. Their history could be traced by associating them with well-defined trends or schools for it would not be possible to attribute to them a common denominator. In short, we are dealing with a critical hypothesis which the critic himself in one part of his work proposes as a theory of complements.[60]

If we try to form a general idea of the methods and trends which prevail in the works just analyzed, we may note that an effort is being made to distinguish between the narrative and legal sections of the Hexateuch and to break away from the custom of assigning to them a common origin. Secondly, an effort is being made in the case of the narrative sections to substitute for the four or five documents of the classic documentary theory of the Pentateuch two basic documents (Deuteronomy forming a literature of its own), viz., the Yahwist and the sacerdotal narrator. As time went on these are supposed to have been expanded, augmented, and practically rewritten as a result of interpolation, glossing, and editorial recast-

---

60. In order that this sketch may be as complete as possible, two more works, of less importance, are cited: Horst, *Das Privilegsrecht Jahwes: Rechtsgeschichtliche Untersuchungen zum Deuteronomium* (Göttingen, 1930) and S. Küchler, *Das Heiligkeitsgesetz, Lev. 17-26: Ein literarkritische Untersuchung* (Königsberg, 1929).

ing. To justify these conclusions, which appear in comparison with the simple solution of the documentary theory very complex, recent writers claim that there are more discrepancies, disagreements, and even antinomies in the Hexateuch narratives than strict followers of Wellhausen have admitted. They argue that the documentary theory cannot account for these manifold discrepancies, because: 1) several of them are of the real, rather than of the literary, lexicographical, or stylistic order and prove the existence of variations in oral tradition antecedent to editing, without supplying any grounds for thinking that the sources were different documents; 2) even when these contradictions concern the literary form, they are often too disparate to serve in the reconstruction of one or several homogeneous documents. They are often *membra disiecta,* betraying the hand of glossarists, or in the case of lengthier passages, the work of interpolators. If they show affinity and connection at times, they lead us at most to admit one editorial influence. Even then they do not permit us to weave a completely new literary fabric.

This school of thought numbers among its adherents some of the writers who were classed in the first edition as members of the Wellhausen group. Among these is Gerhard von Rad, professor at Jena;[61] he still clings, however, to the Wellhausen tradition in holding for the four documents, J E D P, and in claiming that they are represented throughout the Hexateuch. In this he opposes

61. Von Rad: *Das Gottesvolk im Deuteronomium* (Stuttgart, 1929); *Das Geschichtsbild des chronistischen Werkes* (1930); "Die levitische Predigt in den Büchern der Chronik," *Festschrift Procksch* (1934), 113-124; *Die Priesterschrift im Hexateuch* (Stuttgart, 1934); *Das formgeschichtliche Problem des Hexateuchs.*

Noth, for whom the traditions of Gilgal preserved in the Book of Josue are to be separated from those of the Pentateuch. Von Rad likewise follows the classical Wellhausen doctrine in his attitude toward the Elohist, and in so doing dissents from Mowinckel's claim that the document first appears in the second chapter of Genesis. Finally, not only does he keep the sacerdotal cycle of narratives, but he feels that he can break it up into P^1 and P^2. On the other hand, as the previously mentioned conclusions from his latest work show,[62] he abandons classical Wellhausenism completely in his views on the provenience of the documents. By doing this, he falls in with recent trends and accordingly deserves mention in this part of our book. He considers the four documents to be the term of a long development. His growing anti-Wellhausen attitude, furthermore, is evident in his views on the origin of the Hexateuch's general framework and on the cult sources from which it is derived. Far from being a post-Exilic production of Esdras and his circle, the framework of the Hexateuch goes back in its entirety to the Yahwist. Now, the Yahwist is closely related in literary style to the "history of David's lineage," and this history was apparently composed as events occurred. The conclusion seems to follow that the Yahwist account also dates from a little after the reign of David.

Professor von Rad thinks that he can trace it back still further. He distinguishes in the Hexateuch, and also in the Yahwist, since the framework of the Hexateuch derives from it, two cycles of tradition, that of the revelation of God on Sinai and that of Exodus and the conquest of Chanaan. In his opinion, these two cycles obviously

---

62. Cf. *supra,* note 57.

have a close connection with cult. The Sinai cycle is associated with the Feast of Tabernacles, and the Exodus cycle with the profession of faith in Deuteronomy xxvi, 1-11.

For all their importance, these conclusions are not the writer's last word. He adds that the Feast of Tabernacles takes us back to the Yahwistic amphictyony, the historical moment when the tribes of Israel formed a confederation under the ægis of Yahweh. Again, since the traditions of Pentecost are centered about the sanctuary of Gilgal, near Jericho, the origin of the feast takes us back to the time of the division of Chanaan among the various tribes after the conquest.

It is evident from these bold conclusions that von Rad is frankly breaking with the Wellhausen theory and leading us back almost to the traditional stand on the Mosaic origin of Israelite legislation.[63]

Mention has just been made of Moses. Except for Klostermann, the authors cited thus far scarcely considered the second important problem in the critical study of the Pentateuch, namely, the significance of the rôle which Moses played in the composition of the Israelite epic and in the codification of the laws. When they do mention it, they hardly ever think of attributing any notable part of this literature to the man whom tradition names lawgiver of the Hebrews. They all agree, however, in admitting a relative antiquity for Israelite legislation and in considering it in great part of pre-Exilic origin. Eerdmans in particular has returned to the view, prevalent before the time

---

63. Von Rad, *Das formgeschichtliche Problem*, 37, 38, 40, 42, 43, 44.
Cf. *infra* the similar views of A. Alt, from whom von Rad seems to derive.

of Graf and Wellhausen, that the body of Levitical law antedated the promulgation of Deuteronomy (iv, 144).

The question of the Mosaic origin was discussed more explicitly by Harold M. Wiener and Max Löhr. Until his tragic death in an anti-Zionist riot in Jerusalem in 1929, the former kept up an enthusiastic interest in the problem of the Pentateuch. As in the case of many Jewish authors who have not entirely forgotten rabbinical pilpuls, his voluminous work is heterogeneous and somewhat subtle. From it, however, the following capital assertion stands out: The Mosaic Laws were not evolved all of a sudden in some late era of Israelite history. They represent, on the contrary, the treasure of laws, precepts, ordinances, judicial acts, and court sentences that accrued to the Hebrew people from its early days down to the time of Esdras and Nehemias. In its general setting, in many of its dominant ideas, in many legal sections, the Torah goes back to Moses. The laws grew in the course of the years like a snowball, but the name of Moses remains associated with the whole, almost as the name of St. Pius V attaches to the Roman Missal and that of Napoleon to the civil code of Western European nations.

Löhr puts greater stress than does Wiener on the literary activity of Esdras. In this he agrees with critical opinion, but he revives for his own purposes a traditional idea which considers this activity chiefly a matter of editing. The documents collected by Esdras which he developed into the Hexateuch are alleged to have been composed in the main before the Babylonian Exile. Some of them are even dated from the time of Moses. Löhr claims proof of this for the Deuteronomic legislation — but perhaps this choice of a document was not a very happy one!

Briefly, then, Löhr also favors a theory of additions, similar to those of Klostermann, Eerdmans, Volz, and Rudolph. Several recent authors call these hypotheses "crystallization" theories in order to distinguish them from the old theories of complements.

After reading the searching analyses of Löhr and of Eerdmans, it is hard to discover in the Israelite laws anything out of which to reconstruct the four classic documents of Graf's theory. At least it is hard to discover in them a Yahwist code and an Elohist code linking up with the narrative sections of the same name. This fact, as well as the success of form criticism in other fields, has led a few exegetes of recent times to seek new hypotheses and to try out the method of form criticism on the Mosaic Law.[64] Actually, the variety of the terms employed in the Bible to signify laws — *debarîm, mishpatîm,* and *toroth* — seems to invite the quest for as many, if not more, categories of law, distinct in literary character.

The first systematic attempt to classify the laws according to literary forms and not according to the criterion of the divine names, Yahweh and Elohim, was set forth, if the author is not mistaken, in the little work of Anton Jirku, published in 1927. Here the distinction established by Koschacker between *Gesetzeskodex,* legal

---

64. Jirku, *Das weltliche Recht im Alten Testament: Stilgeschichtliche und rechtsvergleichende Studien zu den juristischen Gesetzen des Pentateuchs* (Gütersloh, 1927); A. Jepsen, *Untersuchungen zum Bundesbuch;* Alt, "Die Ursprünge des israelitischen Rechts," *Berichte über die Verhandl. der Sächsischen Akademie der Wissenschaften,* LXXXVI, fasc. 1 (Leipzig, 1934); K. Möhlenbrink, "Die levitischen Ueberlieferungen des Alten Testaments," *ZAW,* XI (1934), 184-230; Begrich, "Die priesterliche Tora," *Werden und Wesen des Alten Testaments, BZAW,* 65, 63-88.

code, and *Rechtsbuch,* collection of laws, is introduced. While a legal code is always drawn up in accordance with a preconceived plan, a collection consists of a material compilation of separate unrelated laws arranged in no special order. If Jirku is correct, most of the collections of laws tracked down in the Pentateuch by literary critics are nothing more than compilations fashioned from the remains of ancient codes. Form criticism would, then, have as its task the reconstitution of these lost *corpora juris.* Jirku, in his effort to reconstruct the ancient codes, was led to distinguish ten literary genera or styles of Israelite legislation. The most ancient of these, he holds, are characterized by the introductory formulae, "If a man" and "Thou shalt." Furthermore, it is among the laws expressed in the conditional form that the greatest number of parallels with laws of the ancient East are met. Jirku concludes that Moses might well have drawn upon laws existing at the time and then composed and promulgated his legal code in its ancient Oriental form.

The system of Jirku was adopted by Albrecht Alt, one of the best of the rising generation of German exegetes. His monograph surpasses by far the work of his predecessor in shrewdness of analysis, closeness of reasoning, and sobriety of conclusion. According to Alt, the ancient law of the Hebrews, from the standpoint of editing, falls into two great classes: laws expressed in the conditional form, which derive from casuistry, and those couched in apodictic form. The latter are differentiated according to six formulae. It is sufficient to compare the two classes to understand what a striking contrast they exhibit.

Casuistic laws, introduced ordinarily by *'îm* ("when") or *kî* ("suppose that"), originated in the local secular courts of justice. These *mishpatîm,* as they are properly called, have nothing specifically Israelitish about them; their "situation in life" is the land of Chanaan, among the Chanaanite tribes that occupied Palestine during the period of the Hyksos. One can even trace further and see in them the ancient Oriental law common to a number of Near Eastern peoples. The Israelite judicature adopted this system of jurisprudence, ratified it, and imposed it on the federated tribes. The Bible itself seems in one place to establish connection between this form of law and Josue and the city of Sichem.

Apodictic laws, which may be called constitutional, appear in an entirely different light both in form and in meaning. Alt cites (p. 41) as a typical example Exodus xxi, 12. Here the "situation in life" appears in most instances specifically Israelite, national and Yahwistic (p. 60). Moreover the solemn tone is superior to the legal phraseology used by ordinary tribunals and in casuistic law (p. 61). The implication, therefore, is that the laws emanate by way of solemn promulgation from religious assemblies such as the one described in Deuteronomy xxvii which was staged in the awe-inspiring amphitheater formed by Mount Ebal and Mount Garizim. Alt thinks that similar solemn promulgations of Yahwistic laws took place at regular intervals, i. e., as Mowinckel suggested, every seven years in autumn at the Feast of the Tabernacles, during which the people renewed their covenant with Yahweh. To these septennial assemblies Alt affirms that the prescription of Deuteronomy xxxi, 10-13 originally applied, adding that nothing prohibits our making the first of these assemblies coincide with the establishment of the covenant of Moses in the desert. As a matter of fact, since Israelite constitutional law is essentially Yahwistic, and Yahwism necessarily takes us back for its origin to the sojourn in the desert, this law traces back to Moses and his influence over the tribes.[65]

Alt's study is only an essay, but it is full of promise. He should continue his researches along the lines he has marked out and carry them into the sphere of the other laws, especially that of the sacerdotal *toroth*.

This phase of the work was recently taken up by Begrich, who published his first findings in *Werden und Wesen des Alten Testaments*. Up to the present they give no clue to the author's historical conclusions.

The present author has, therefore, indicated how the anti-Wellhausen reactions have challenged three cardinal hypotheses of the documentary theory of the Hexateuch: the existence of the second Elohist, the relative and absolute chronology of Deuteronomy, and the integral post-Exilic origin of the Priestly Code. It may be added that a fourth hypothesis is undermined — the assertion that the books of Chronicles are peculiarly partisan in character. Here, also, we seem to be on the eve of a shift of critical positions which will effect the repudiation of the classical

---

65. The conclusions formulated by Jepsen (*loc. cit.*) seem to the present author less fortunate. He distinguishes four classes of laws: 1) the Hebrew *mishpatîm* introduced by the conjunction, *'im;* 2) three collections of laws, not Hebraic but Israelite: a) *mishpatîm* introduced by a participial verb, b) laws of morality, and c) cult laws. He thus makes a distinction between Israelite and Hebrew tradition; the two are supposed to have been combined by the priests of Yahweh a short time before the establishment of the kingdom in order to promote the fusion of the Chanaanite Hebrews with the Israelites.

Wellhausen attitude toward these books and the vindication, in great part, of their historical value.[66]

III. APPROACHES TO A NEW SYNTHESIS OF THE HISTORY OF ISRAEL

Having set forth to the best of his ability the new literary conclusions, the author still has one last task, the most important and also the most precarious: that of extracting from numerous publications that general synthesis of the religious history of Israel which may, perhaps, be adopted one day in independent circles. This task is difficult because of the abundance of material, the frequent disagreements between writers, the elusiveness of general trends. There is the risk of sketching a purely subjective picture, of conjuring up a school of exegetes which exists only in the pages here devoted to it. The attempt is, then, necessarily somewhat arbitrary: scattered information is collected; separated members are assembled and dislo-

---

66. Cited here for various reasons are Schaeder, *Esra der Schreiber*, and *Iranische Beiträge*, I (1930); Millar Burrows, "The Origin of Neh. 3, 33-37," *AJSL*, LII (1935-1936), 235-244 and "Nehemiah's Tour of Inspection," *BASOR*, 64 (1936), 11 ff.; see also *AASOR*, XIV (1934), 115-140, and *JBL* (1935), 29-39; von Rad, "Die levitische Predigt," *loc. cit.*; Galling, "Der Tempelschatz nach Berichten und Urkunden im Buche Esra," *Zeitschrift des Deutschen Palästina-Vereins*, LX (1937), 177-183; M. Noth, "Eine siedlungsgeographische Liste in I Chron. 2 und 4," *ibid.*, LV (1932), pp. 97-124; J. Hänel, "Das Recht des Opferschlachtens in der chronistischen Literatur," *ZAW*, XIV (1937), 46-67; J. Göttsberger, *Die Bücher der Chronik oder Paralipomenon*, Die Heilige Schrift des Alten Testaments ser. (Bonn, 1939); B. Luther, "Kahal und 'Edah als Hilfsmittel der Quellenscheidung im Priestercodex und in der Chronik," *ZAW*, XV (1938), 44-63; Noordtzij, *Kronieken*, I-II (Kampen, 1937-1938); A. van Selms, *I Kronieken* (Groningen, 1939); Welch, *The Work of the Chronicler: Its Purpose and Its Date*, Schweich Lectures ser. (London, 1939). On the four last-mentioned authors, read the present author's *Chronique d'Ancien Testament*, 17-20.

cated joints, so to speak, forced back into place, in the hope that a spark of vital reality will give them life.

The conclusions of this final process will be placed under the three headings of political, religious, and literary history.

It is worth repeating that since the appearance of the last original work by Wellhausen on the Old Testament (1895), the political history of the Hebrews has undergone a truly remarkable transformation. Its background has been quite changed. Henceforth along the historical horizon of the ancient East parade the civilizations of Babylon and Assyria, beginning with Hammurabi. Egypt and Syria follow. So too does Palestine, especially the Palestine of the Tell-el-Amarna era. Soon afterward, the civilization of Phœnicia appears, living once again in the Ras Shamra tablets. Then the culture of the Aramean Mesopotamia to the north, preserved for us in the archives of Mari. The change has also been considerable in the more limited region of Palestine. Archæological excavations have made it possible for us to grasp the remarkable interplay of influences at work in this land of passage from the time of the wars of conquest under the twelfth dynasty of Egypt — one thinks of the curious history of the travels of Sinuhe the Egyptian — down to the time of Christ. Even within the historical cycles through which the Israelites passed from the fifteenth to the first century B. C., we would still have to take account of several new opinions that have received recognition. The author must content himself here with the enumeration of a few key conclusions. Such are the historical resurrection of Moses, if it may be so titled,[67] and the return to the limelight of other figures, especially Samuel and David, whom Wellhausen had held to be of minor importance; the new outlook in regard to King Josias and the reform attributed to him; the more conservative appraisal of the repercussions which the Babylonian Exile had on the origins of monotheistic, Messianic, and eschatological beliefs; and lastly, the new ideas on the activity of Esdras and Nehemias in the reconstruction of the Jewish community of Jerusalem and in what is called the birth of Judaism.[68]

---

67. On the achievement of Moses, read Volz, *Mose und sein Werk* (Tübingen, 1907; 2nd ed., Tübingen, 1932); Gressmann, *Mose und seine Zeit* (1913); Böhl, "Moses en zijn werk," reprint from *Internationaal Christendom* (1934); L. Köhler, "Der Dekalog," *TR,* I (1929), 161-184; Baumgartner, "Der Kampf um das Deuteronomium," *ibid.,* I, 7-25; Lods, "Israelitische Opfervorstellungen und -bräuche," *ibid.,* III (1931), 347-366; Caspari, "Neuere Versuche geschichtswissenschaftlicher Vergewisserung über Mose," *ZAW,* new ser., I (1924), 297-313; T. C. Vriezen, "Litterair-historische Vragen aangaande de Decaloog," *NTS,* XXII (1939), 1-24, 34-51.

68. On the history of Israel, see note 42, and the critical bibliography of Pfeiffer cited in note 43. For Germany, special mention should be made of the numerous publications of Professors Alt and Noth, several of which open up truly new vistas on the history of Palestine: Alt, *Die Landname der Israeliten in Palästina* (Leipzig, 1925), *Die Staatenbildung der Israeliten in Palästina* (Leipzig, 1930), "Die Rolle Samariens bei der Entstehung des Judentums," *Festschrift Procksch* (Leipzig, 1934), *Völker und Staaten Syriens im frühen Altertum* (Leipzig, 1936); Noth, *Das System der zwölf Stämme Israels* (Stuttgart, 1930). Mention should also be made of the copious documentation assembled in A. H. Godbey, *Premosaic Hebrew Religion: Inductive Outline for Students* (Durham, N. C., 1935), and especially his *New Light on the Old Testament* (3rd ed., Durham, 1936). Of less importance but animated by the same spirit are: Alt, "Judas Gaue unter Josia," *Palästina Jahrbuch,* XXI, (1925), 100-116, and "Das System der Stammesgrenzen im Buche Josua," *Sellin Festschrift* (1927), 13-24; K. Elliger, "Die dreissig Helden Davids," *PJ,* XXXI (1935), 29-75; Alt, "Zur Geschichte der Grenzen zwischen Judäa and Samaria," *ibid.,* and "Josua," *Werden und Wesen des Alten Testaments* (Berlin, 1936), 13-26; Montgomery, "Archival Data in the Book of Kings," *JBL* (1934) 46-52; Lods, "Les Fouilles d'Aï et l'époque de l'entrée des Israélites en Palestine," *Mélanges Cumont* (Brussels, 1936), 847-857. In addition, all the issues of the *Palästina Jahrbuch,* in which Alt has published many articles of his own and of his collaborators, should be consulted. See also Noth, "Das Buch Josua," *Handbuch zum Alten Testament,* ed. Eissfeldt (Tübingen, 1938), which avails itself of

The abandonment of the old standpoints and strategic positions is much less in evidence in the religious history of the Chosen People. The landscape here presents more hills and valleys; the air is foggier; the colors are fainter; conditions of visibility are poor, especially for the eye of the inexperienced. But once the mist clears away, it is astonishing to see how much ground has been covered since the days of Wellhausen. Those events in Israel's religious history on which Wellhausen criticism based its synthesis have been called into question. This refers particularly to the reform of Josias, the supposed "planism" of Ezechiel (xl-xlviii), the aftermath of the catastrophe of the Exile, the splendor of the Second Temple, and the dynamic influence of Esdras and Nehemias. It is no longer held that the religious history of Israel was governed by forces centering about two poles, prophetism and the levitical priesthood. Alongside these factors, of which neither the existence nor the often predominant rôle is denied, others, more obscure, more unpretentious, more forgotten, but no less effective, have been discovered. Among these may be cited the faith of the common people, the influence of foreign religions by way of direct ascendency or of reaction, the reforming activities of religious groups, such as Levites, Rechabites, Nebiîm (sons of the prophets), and doubtless still other forces which have not as yet come to notice.[69]

---

several results given in the above-mentioned publications. It is to be understood, of course, that not everything in these studies can be approved: they contain many subjective elements, but they do sponsor a different method and breathe a different spirit from what the old school of criticism had to offer.

69. See, for example, J. M. P. Smith, "Southern Influences upon Hebrew Prophecy," *AJSL,* XXXV (1918), 1-19, and "The Effect of the Disruption on the Hebrew Thought of God," *ibid.,* XXXII (1916), 261-269; L. Köhler, "Alttestamentliche Theologie," *TR,* VII (1935), 255-276, and VIII (1936), 55-69, 247-284.

Furthermore, relations between the priests and the prophets appear to have been less strained than the Wellhausen school thought; or, to be more exact, it is now evident that intermediary groups existed, principally those of priests and cantors who were also endowed with prophetic inspiration. Lastly, attention has been called to other sources of polarization and tension, such as the opposition between the Northern and Southern Kingdoms, between the central sanctuary at Jerusalem and the local shrines, between the Messianic aspirations of the religious circles and the laicism of the royal power.[70]

As for literary history, the present author simply admits that it is the field in which he personally finds it most difficult to grasp the main lines of development. Perhaps he is not wrong in giving as its most characteristic traits: first, disgust for the process of excessive parceling out of the text — critical plum-pudding and pemmican are out of style; second, a tendency to divide the literary deposits of the Old Testament, less along the horizontal plane of chronological succession than along the vertical, i. e., according to a more or less synchronological elaboration of various parallel traditions. Wellhausen adhered tenaciously to the chronological order of prophets first, then Law. Today, the trend is to admit, up to a certain point, that the Law and the prophets are two distinct lodes

---

70. One of the works providing the best information on the new light under which the cultural and religious history of Israel is beginning to be viewed is unquestionably that of J. Pedersen, *Israel: Its Life and Culture* (Oxford, 1926). See also J. Kaufmann, "Probleme der israelitisch-jüdischen Religionsgeschichte," *ZAW*, VII (1930), 23-43; Pedersen, "Die Auffassung vom Alten Testament," *ibid.*, VII, 161-181; Eissfeldt, "Zwei Leidener Darstellungen der israelitischen Religionsgeschichte (Kuenen-Eerdmans)," *ZDMG*, LXXXV (1931), 172-195.

running back independently to the sources of Mosaic Yahwism itself.

For the parallel literary deposits thus distinguished there is relatively little effort at ascertaining authors. Preference is given to determining the locale of provenience — schools, sanctuaries, political or cultural circles. In other words, the "situation in life" which brought the writings into existence and nourished them with its own substance is being investigated. That the early beginnings of each of these deposits goes back much further than Wellhausen imagined is freely admitted. Even Eissfeldt has not hesitated to draw this last conclusion, for he elected to write for each of the Wellhausen documents what he calls their pre-history.[71]

Nothing provides a better understanding of the actual development of, and the approach to, the new history of Israel now being worked out than does a careful perusal of certain works to which attention has already been drawn. With the reader's permission, he is referred to the views of Welch, Böhl, Oesterley-Robinson, and even of von Rad and Hempel, on the formation of Hebrew laws; to the syntheses of the religious history of Israel by Eerdmans, Volz, Mowinckel, and Meek; to the histories of Israel by R. Kittel, Sellin, Jirku and Lods; and to the numerous works already published by a particularly active exegete, Professor Causse of the University of

---

71. Eissfeldt, *Einleitung*, 8-168. See also Baumgartner, "Wellhausen und der heutige Stand der alttestamentlichen Wissenschaft," *TR*, II (1930), 287-307, and "Alttestamentliche Einleitung und Literaturgeschichte," *ibid.*, VIII (1936), 179-222; R. Abramowski, "Vom Streit um das Alte Testament," *ibid.*, IX (1937), 65-93.

Strassburg.[72] These works reflect faithfully the fluctuations of critical thought and give a clear idea of the creative forces that are at present busy with the exegesis of the Old Testament even in the case of writers who still retain much of Wellhausenism. In the main we are still in the midst of confusion and change; but it may be said that in the end order, as always, will emerge from chaos.[73]

CONCLUSION

In the past thirty odd years, critical studies parallel to, if not in opposition to, the Wellhausen theory have been

---

72. Welch, *Deuteronomy: The Framework to the Code* (London, 1932). On this author's work, see chapter I, note 61. Böhl, *Genesis I,* (2nd ed., Groningen, 1930), 11-20; Oesterley-Robinson, *An Introduction to the Books of the Old Testament.* See the stemma of the documents according to the Oesterley-Robinson theory, given in Coppens, *En marge de l'Histoire sainte,* 13. Eerdmans, *De Godsdienst van Israël;* Meek, *Hebrew Origins;* Lods, *Israel from Its Beginnings to the Middle of the Eighth Century.* Causse, listed in the first chapter among the proponents of the Wellhausen theory because of certain aspects of his work, also finds a place here. He represents in France the dynamism of the Gunkel-Gressmann-Mowinckel school. His output is already imposing: *Les Pauvres d'Israël: Prophètes, psalmistes, messianistes* (1922); *Israël et la vision de l'humanité* (1924); *Les plus vieux chants de la Bible* (1926); *Les origines de la Diaspora et son rôle dans la formation du judaïsme* (1929); *Du groupe ethnique à la communauté religieuse. Le Problème sociologique de la religion d'Israël* (1937).

73. A series of articles by F. Dornseiff against the Wellhausen system might be mentioned: "Antikes zum Alten Testament: I. Genesis," *ZAW,* XI (1934), 57-75; "II. Exodos," *ibid.,* XII (1935), 153-171; "III. Levitikon," *ibid.,* XIV (1937), 127-136; "IV. Die Abfassungszeit des Pentateuchs und die Deuteronomiumfrage," XV (1938), 64-85. Cf. also the same author's "Hesiods Tage und Werke und das Morgenland," *Philologus* (1934), 397-415; "Das Buch Prediger," *ZDMG,* LXXXIX (1935), 243-249; "Aegyptische Liebeslieder, Hoheslied, Sappho, Theokrit," *ibid.,* XL (1936), 589-601. These articles show originality in seeking to establish points of contact between the Old Testament and the Greek world; however, the conclusions drawn seem too little substantiated for the work of Dornseiff to merit more than honorable mention in a footnote.

numerous and important. Several of the results may be considered as definitely established, even though these researches have not as yet won the general recognition they deserve. Some reason for this comparative unsuccess may be discerned in the fact that the new methods have not produced a work of synthesis that could stand as their definite representative, as the work of Wellhausen stood in the sanctum of the classical school of critics. The histories of Israel published by Sellin and R. Kittel have, of course, been quite successful but their authors failed to take a determined stand on the fundamental questions which the new methods raise. As for the literary history of Hempel, the present writer has already expressed his great esteem of it. But it is only a sketch, and moreover falls a little short in erudition.[74] Perhaps the ideal work of synthesis will never be written. It is always easier to risk a few hypotheses, to look at facts in the glow of a luminous idea, than to burrow for the truth, which is infinitely complex, and especially so in the field of history. Seekers for truth cannot be guilty of one-track-mindedness, but must renounce that well-worn trick of propaganda, excessive simplification. The *simplex veri sigillum* can, perhaps, find an application to the fine points of metaphysical speculation, but it is justifiable much less frequently when applied to the complex life of nations and individuals.

---

74. R. Kittel, *Die alttestamentliche Wissenschaft in ihren wichtigsten Ergebnissen;* Lods, *op. cit.;* A. T. Olmstead, *History of Palestine and Israel to the Macedonian Conquest* (New York, 1931), and cf. Albright, *art. cit.,* JQR, XXIV (1934), 363-376; Kittel, *Geschichte des Volkes Israel* (7th ed., Stuttgart, 1932), 3 vols.; Sellin, *Geschichte des israelitisch-jüdischen Volkes* (1924-1932), 2 vols.; T. H. Robinson, *A History of Israel* (2nd ed., Oxford, 1934), 2 vols.

It would be wrong, however, to end on a discouraging note. Let it be said, rather, that the harvesting of new facts is not yet complete. The exegetes have not, perhaps, finished winnowing the wheat with which they have filled the barns of Biblical science in the course of the last thirty years.

CHAPTER THREE

THE FUTURE

HAD it been desired to select catch headings for these chapters, the first might have been entitled, "Where do we come from?", because in it were traced the broad outlines of the development of Old Testament historical criticism; the second, which studied the chief reactions to the Wellhausen theory and new departures in criticism before and after the war of 1914-1918, might have been labeled, "Where are we?"; while this third and last chapter would have to be headed by "Where are we going?", because it aims at drawing lessons from what has happened — it is never too late to do good or to profit by the teaching of the past — and at suggesting norms for future research.[1]

---

1. For the bibliography, see the numerous references throughout the preceding chapters, and also:

From the Protestant or the independent viewpoint: J. Battersby Harford, "Since Wellhausen," *The Expositor,* ser. IX, V (July-December, 1925), 4-26, 83-102, 164-182, 244-265, 323-349, 403-429; Löhr, "Zum Hexateuchproblem," *OLZ,* XXIX (1926), 4-13; E. König, *Der doppelte Wellhausenianismus im Lichte meiner Quellenforschungen* (Gütersloh, 1927); Peake, "Recent Development in Old Testament Criticism," reprint from the *John Rylands Library Bulletin* (Manchester, University Press, 1928); Kittel, *Die alttestamentliche Wissenschaft in ihren wichtigsten Ergebnissen;* Böhl, "Hoofdvragen aangaande het Oude Testament," *NTS,* XIII (1930), 193-205, 225-238; E. König, *Ist die moderne Pentateuchkritik auf Tatsachen begründet? Zur Beleuchtung allerneuester Behauptungen* (Stuttgart, 1933); Lofthouse, "The Evolution of Religion in the Old Testament," *Modern Churchman,* XXIV (1934), 259-274; T. H. W. Maxwell, "The Evolution of Judaism in the Post-Exilic Period," *ibid.,* 275-294; Cook, "Biblical Criticism and the Interpretation of His-

111

Before entering on particulars, it is desirable to glance back in summary over the ground covered.

Suppose that Julius Wellhausen were to return to the world in this year of grace and were to inspect once again the chantier of Old Testament criticism. He would find things changed very much, perhaps beyond recognition, from what they were in 1895, when he quit the field proclaiming to all who had ears to hear that the job was completely finished. The books of the Old Testament have once again become the scene of extensive operations, in which the demolishers of the Wellhausen hypothesis are almost as numerous as the defenders. The linking up of the Old Testament with the ancient East on the one hand and with the New Testament on the other has not been realized, at least not in the sense in which the talented historian thought he could achieve it.

When the school of Wellhausen was at the zenith of its success, it gloried in the enthusiasm of its coryphæus and the irrepressible zeal of his loyal assistants and followers. More than once, we know, it was accused of a lack of reserve, and was reminded of the dictum of Horace: "Est quadam prodire tenus, si non datur ultra"; but disdaining its adversaries, it retorted:

---

tory," *ibid.*, XXVI (1936-1937), 183-194; Hölscher, "Johannes Pedersen 'Israel,'" *Theol. Stud. Krit.*, CVIII (1937-1938), 234-262.

From the Catholic viewpoint: Bea, "Der heutige Stand der Pentateuchfrage," *Bi*, XVI (1935), 175-200; M. J. Lagrange, "L'authenticité mosaïque de la Genèse et la théorie des documents," *RB*, XLVII (1938), 162-183; Coppens, "De nieuwe Koers van de onafhankelijke Oudtestamentische Bijbelkritiek," *Ons Geloof*, XXVI (1940), 49-69.

From the Jewish viewpoint: E. Urbach, "Neue Wege der Bibelwissenschaft," *Monatsschrift für Geschichte und Wissenschaft des Judentums*, LXXXII (Breslau, 1938), 1-22. The author discusses the first volume of J. Kaufmann's Hebrew work, *Histoire de la Foi israélite depuis les origines jusqu'à la fin du second Temple* (Tel Aviv, n. d.).

"Bescheidenheit ist eine Zier
Doch weiter kommt man ohne ihr."

Today, the advocates of moderation and conservatism have
their revenge and to some extent can enjoy victory. Old
Testament criticism is happily rid of the pontifical tone of
Wellhausen, and above all of a band of enthusiastic
epigoni. Even those who remain faithful to classical
Wellhausenism "in order not to flounder in uncertainty
once again," and who, accordingly, banish like so many
evil thoughts the misgivings of Klostermann, Löhr,
Eerdmans, Volz, Rudolph, and Welch, admit that the
structure reared by the master is full of weak spots, and
when tested by the most delicate instruments appears ready
to topple from its exposed and shaken foundation.

We have every reason to be glad of the lesson in
modesty and cautious reserve that history has thus inflicted
on writers who were too sure of themselves and too presumptuous.[2] We can be glad also that the best independent exegetes are beginning to insist once again on the
elementary precepts of historical method. "Let us distrust
our ideas," writes G. Lanson, "and take care that nothing
in them goes beyond the limits of established fact." And
Fontenelle asserts, not without a touch of exaggeration:
"In the sciences, all conjectures have an equal right to be
formed and often have hardly any right to dispute the
field."[3]

---

2. *"Ein einz'ges Aktenstück kann alles umgestalten!"*
3. On the notion of history and the limitations of historical research, see: R. G. Collingwood, "Human Nature and Human History,"
Proceedings of the British Academy, XXII (1936), 97-127; R. Aron,
*Introduction à la Philosophie de l'Histoire: Essai sur les limites de
l'objectivité historique* (Paris, 1939).

However, the sense of satisfaction should not become overweening—especially in those who profit by the victory after having expended little or no energy in the struggle. This feeling of exuberant triumph is conspicuous among certain conservative Protestant writers, especially archæologists, who exploit the most insignificant discoveries in order to draw from them on the spot confirmation of some Biblical datum, or worse still, proof of some ultra-conservative exegetical thesis. More frequently than not, taking their hopes for realities, they are hasty in their conclusions and betray a woeful lack of critical acumen. There come to mind the fantastic notices appearing regularly in the sensational sections of the English and American press and, on occasion, reproduced — often in garbled form — in continental newspapers, even Catholic ones. Only the great journals, such as *Le Temps* and *Le Journal des Débats,* seek accurate information in these matters and get it at first hand from the learned societies and academies. There come to mind also the publications of certain archæologists, or of their patrons and sponsors. Such, for instance, are some of the productions of Woolley, intended for the general public, and the little work of Sir Charles Marston, *The Bible Is True.*[4] It is dangerous to try to adapt to the framework of the latest archæological conclusions this or that Biblical episode, for example, the story of paradise, or of the deluge, or even of happenings much nearer to us in time, such as the call of Abraham.

It is the present author's desire, therefore, to appraise from a more objective standpoint and, if the phrase is not considered presumptuous, with more equanimity, the contributions of Oriental archæology and of the new methods

---

4. Sir Charles Marston, *The Bible Is True* (London, 1934).

of literary criticism. The aim is less to publish a proclama-
tion of victory than to draw up a strict inventory and reach
an exact balancing of accounts. Inaccurate balance sheets
are useless. Hence, two questions will be considered:
What is the condition of Old Testament historical criticism after the various reactions it has provoked? And
what can the attitude of Catholic exegesis be in the face
of these reactions and of the partial failure of classical
Wellhausenism?

I. THE PRESENT POSITION OF OLD TESTAMENT
HISTORICAL CRITICISM

What, then, of the Wellhausen front line in view of
the gaps torn in it by the reactions sketched in the foregoing pages? To read some Wellhausen critics, one might
suppose their position untouched. Such is the opinion, expressed with variations of course, of A. S. Peake, Eduard
König, and J. Battersby Harford. It is also the view
adopted in a modified form by Lofthouse.[5] Consequently,
if a just judgment is to be passed on the present situation
of Wellhausenism, it will be necessary once again to distinguish in the Wellhausen achievement three fundamental
aspects, the historical, the religious, and the literary.

From the standpoint of the history of Israel, we have
seen that the classical Wellhausen system is shattered.
What can it oppose to the archæological data with which
exploration in the Near East has enriched man's knowledge? The facts to which these pages have called attention
are in great measure definitely established, and they de-

5. Lofthouse, *loc. cit.* See the excerpt quoted *supra,* 49.

stroy forever the Wellhausen conception of the Israelites as a primitive people, cut off from other nations and animated by a religious impulse powerful yet purely natural, and all their own.

From the standpoint of the religious history of Israel, it may be affirmed that at least the basic Wellhausen positions are out of date. This was established in the preceding chapter by exposing the shortcomings of the evolutional scheme offered by the Wellhausen school to explain the unique religious position in the Near East of the people of Israel. Comparative study, far from having cast doubt on the uniqueness and transcendency of the religion of Israel, has placed them in more striking relief. The *Einzigartigkeit,* or exceptional nature, of that religion is such that it is in no wise explained by merely natural forces, and certainly not by the social and political factors to which the Wellhausen school appealed. Accordingly, to account for the transcendency of Israel's religion, the more moderate independent critics are returning to the theory of a succession of extraordinary religious experiences, beginning with that of Moses. They even venture to consider these experiences mystical. Now, anyone can see that this is either sidestepping the issue — for how explain that experiences of this sort took place exclusively in Israel and, what is more, in a remarkably continuous and progressive manner? — or else it is drawing singularly close to the traditional supernatural explanation. For this reason some critics go so far as to say: "Science no longer objects to considering the religion of Israel superior to all the religions of antiquity, nor to assigning to its determining factors the name of mystery or what believers may prefer to interpret as a historical miracle."

We have seen how other theses are likewise questioned. Since, however, the history of the Israelite religion is intimately bound up with the history of Biblical literature, we must now turn our attention to the latter. It is here, to repeat, that it is most difficult to form a broad estimate. Certainly, large salients have been driven into the front line of classical Wellhausen literary opinions, but whether this front has actually been broken or not remains to be determined.

For greater clearness, let us recall once more the main aspects of the literary history of the people of Israel. Let us, moreover, distinguish between historical criticism and exegesis, properly so-called, and try to reach a decision on the key points of historical criticism. These include the composition of the Pentateuch, the literary and historical relation between the Law and the prophetical writings, the literary origins of the Messianic and eschatological prophecies, and the historical provenience of the Psalter. Several of these questions have already been touched on in the preceding chapter, but we must return to them for a last review and a final judgment.

Appraisal of the criticisms passed on the classical system of Wellhausen exegesis need not be lengthy. These criticisms may be accepted almost in their entirety. The commentaries of the Wellhausen school are coldly intellectual productions, only too often lacking in æsthetic and religious understanding. On the other hand, the soul of Israel, more than that of any other ancient nation, was a delicate instrument from which issued, under the fingers of the Divine Lutanist, most harmonious and touching chords. When we put aside the Wellhausen commentaries and take up one or other of the leading productions of the Gunkel-Gressmann school, we are fascinated by the breath of life that has passed into Biblical criticism because of the humanism of these authors. It is impossible to forget the profound emotion experienced upon first acquaintance with Gunkel's commentary on the Psalms. What freshness of outlook, of ideas, of sentiments there is in this remarkable achievement, especially when it is compared with certain productions of the school of *Stubenphilologen!* Between the narrow-minded Wellhausen critics and those of the new type there are the wide differences which, to apply an expression of Abel Bonnard, mark off the ant-philologist from the bee-philologist. True, even with the work of the new exegetes, we are far from what believers desire and expect of a commentary on a sacred book. Yet so many excellent observations and such a religious tone are found that one is tempted to lament that their like is not more often met with among ourselves.

It has already been intimated that, in regard to the literary history properly so-called, the present author is not in a position to form a general estimate. It will be most useful, therefore, to group the following remarks according to the principal categories already distinguished in the Old Testament. The proportions of the present work demand that conclusions be presented in a slightly abridged form and in an order perhaps a bit too schematic.

It has been shown in the previous chapters how fundamental the question of the Hexateuch is in Old Testament criticism, because of the complexity of the problems it raises, the implications of the solutions it suggests, and the numerous and violent reactions it has provoked.

Once again, consequently, a little more space must be devoted to it than to other questions. Here, then, reduced to a few theses are the positions around which a new critical theory tends to develop.

The documentary hypothesis, while continuing to exert a powerful attraction, has undergone as a result of critical advance several modifications:

1) In the present arrangement of the Hexateuch, the narrative and legislative sections are more or less closely interwoven. Contrary to the Wellhausen belief, however, there is nothing to prove that any literary connections existed from the beginning between the two groups. It therefore seems very ill-advised to try to find in the two groups exactly the same sources.[6] Critics also are rather presumptuous in looking for the same sources outside the Hexateuch.[7]

2) Even if only the purely narrative sections are considered, the presence of the four classic documents, J E D P, is doubtful. Only the Yahwistic and sacerdotal histories clearly stand out in the present arrangement and possess a specific character and unity that can be sufficiently substantiated. The contention that the Second Elohist is a distinct document has been, we have seen, much disputed, and this point therefore must remain questionable until new and better proofs are forthcoming.[8] Again, the Deuteronomist, if he is admitted, is virtually limited to Deuteronomy and the Book of Josue, so that

---

6. Canon Van Hoonacker himself expressed doubts about the supposed links between the narrative sections and the laws. See Coppens, *Le chanoine Albin Van Hoonacker*, 71-2. See also Eerdmans, *Das Buch Exodus*, 146; and Morgenstern, *The Oldest Document of the Hexateuch*, reprint from *HUCA*, IV (1927).

7. Lagrange, *loc. cit.*, especially 178-9.

8. See Volz and Rudolph, note 58 of chapter II.

the supposed recension of the Hexateuch as a whole is questioned by several writers.

3) In spite of the efforts of critics to establish the homogeneity of these documents and to determine their literary provenience, these points still remain quite obscure. Even among the critics who provisionally cling to the documents, several attribute them to schools rather than to individual authors. Some, notably the Dutch critic Böhl, even think that the symbols represent not so much documents, properly so called, as different recensions which grouped and classified the oral and written traditions bequeathed to the ancient Hebrews. It might be better to consider the written traditions thus obtained as a sort of medium between documents and fragments. They are actually so numerous and heterogeneous that it might even be better to class them as mere fragments.[9] Editorial glossing and interpolation might account for various traditions appearing in the same narrative, not as two or three accounts more or less complete and juxtaposed, but as little clippings much reduced and widely scattered, their mass forming a curious conglomeration, mosaic, or checkerboard. In the documentary theory, on the contrary, such procedure would be difficult or even impossible.[10] Can we imagine editors practically scissoring the texts and then piecing the clippings together like a jig-saw puzzle in

---

9 Böhl, *Genesis* (2nd ed., Groningen, 1930), 2 vols.; and *Exodus* (Groningen, 1925).

10. It is interesting to recall the experience of the Hellenist, Tournier: "Having started out with finding in the *Ajax* of Sophocles passages unworthy of the great poet, he ended up by rejecting the entire tragedy, and died doubting the authenticity of all seven of the Sophoclean plays and begging pardon of God and men for having edited spurious classical tragedies." In 1913, Monsignor Duchesne reminded Loisy of this story. See Loisy, *George Tyrrell et Henri Bremond* (Paris, 1936), 204; and J. Lebreton, "Foi dogmatique et religion mystique: A propos des derniers livres de M. Loisy," *Études*, CCXXX (1937), 204.

order to reconstruct as far as possible a more or less coherent account?[11]

4) To pass on from the narrative sections to the collections of law contained in the Hexateuch: here the positions of the documentary school are even more unstable. Undoubtedly, there is agreement in admitting a group of Deuteronomic laws and another group, equally important, originating in priestly circles. But is it proper to consider the sacerdotal *toroth* as a single, mammoth literary work that can be split up into three basic documents, the Law of Holiness, the Priestly Code properly so called, and the Sacerdotal History? Eerdmans, for instance, definitely questions the existence of the Law of Holiness and the Sacerdotal History. In his opinion, the collections as we have them represent rather a literary warehouse wherein were accumulated and stored as time went on the numerous cult laws elaborated in the sacerdotal and levitical schools. This explains why they are all couched in the same style. It is, of course, well known that the style of a school is handed down from generation to generation, especially where it is transmitted within closed circles.

The Elohistic and Yahwistic Codes are entities whose connection with the Yahwist and the Elohist of the classical Wellhausen school seems more and more problematical. The attempts made to identify them do not appear to have been successful. On what does the identification of the Law of the Covenant and Elohistic Law rest? We cannot rest satisfied that in Exodus xxxiv, 10-26,

---

11. Critics have attempted to justify the process by referring to various similar cases, such as the composition of the *Diatessaron* and the methods of ancient Arabian historiography. Thus Löhr, Eissfeldt, and Bevan. Eissfeldt very recently called attention to another instance in "Hegel-Kritik und Pentateuchkritik," *Th Bl,* XVII (1938), col. 33-41.

we have the Yahwist Code that the Wellhausen theory requires. Consequently, though the majority of critics holds for the presence of several collections of laws and generally clings to the Wellhausen divisions, a growing phalanx of writers refuses to distribute the two codes among the four documents of the Graf school, and instead seeks to discover other sources for them.[12]

Next comes the second critical problem of the Hexateuch, the Mosaic origin of the Israelite epic and laws. From what has just been said, as well as from the previous chapter, it follows that the Wellhausen thesis has on this point also suffered serious assaults. In its radical and intransigent form the thesis really no longer exists. Nevertheless, our Catholic fellow-workers must not delude themselves about the tenor of the new theories. Those especially who are naturally inclined toward conservative positions should recall Monsignor Battifol's maxim, "Nothing is so bold as being conservative." The school of comparative history does not think of attributing to Moses the various codes which the critical method and

---

12. Several instances of the new method of argumentation which, for example, points to the diversity of sanctuaries to explain the diversity of laws, can be found in the works of Welch, Oesterley-Robinson, Böhl, and Löhr. According to Welch, Bb (*Bundesbuch:* Law of the Covenant) is linked with Qadesh, Sichem, and Silo; H (*Heiligkeitsgesetz:* Minor Law of Holiness), with the sanctuary at Jerusalem; D (Deuteronomy), with the code of the Ephraimite prophets; Po (Priestly Code, *Opfertorah*), with the laws of the levitical priesthood. According to Oesterley-Robinson, E and D derive from the sanctuaries of the north; H and the Code of Ezechiel are connected with Jerusalem; P is a compromise between the north and the south with a marked leaning toward H and Ezechiel. According to Böhl, Exodus xx, 1-17, is Sinaitic; Exodus xxxiv, 10-26, comes from Qadesh-Barnea; xx, 20-xxiii, 33, from Gilgal-Sichem (see Jos. xxiv, 25-26); Exodus xxv-xxxi and xxxv-xl, from Silo. According to Löhr, the Laws derive either from the sanctuary of the Ark or from that of the tent of the Covenant; in the latter case, they are connected with Qadesh and form the Book of Deuteronomy.

form criticism distinguish in the Hexateuch. Some writers, however, assign to Moses the substance of the Hexateuch, that is, the fundamental institutions of Mosaism including the Decalogue; the general literary framework of the laws and especially the allusions to the desert and the 'Ark of the Covenant; the essential terminology; and even a quite considerable number of particular laws of the various types contained in ancient Israelite legislation — constitutional or national, civil, penal, liturgical, and sacerdotal — although how many of them are to be attributed to Moses is not stated.[13]

For a rough estimate of the civil laws promulgated by Moses, it is asserted that the Book of the Covenant and its prophetical edition, Deuteronomy, can be of aid. The more ancient sacerdotal laws must be reconstructed, with more or less certainty, on the basis of Exodus xxv-xxxi, xxxv-xl and Leviticus xvii-xxvii, and i-xvi, wherein are to be found the Minor Law of Holiness, the Law of Sacrifices, and the Laws of Purification and Atonement.

Lastly, in this matter of laws, critics, even the most conservative, should not lose sight of the prudent remarks of Fustel de Coulanges. "It is not in the nature of law," he says, "to be absolute and immutable. It changes and develops just as any human institution does. Each society has its code, formed and evolved step by step with its own growth and change, always following the lead of its institutions, its customs, and its beliefs."[14]

---

13. On the Decalogue, the masterpiece of Moses, see henceforth the well-constructed summary articles of Vriezen, listed in chapter II, note 67. On the antiquity of the general scheme of the Hexateuch, read von Rad, *Das formgeschichtliche Problem des Hexateuchs*.

14. N. D. Fustel de Coulanges, *La Cité antique* (Paris, Hachette, n. d.), chapter viii, 363-4.

Although the Mosaic origin of the greater part of Israelite law is asserted only with notable reservations, many critics are now adopting the hypothesis of a pre-Exilic origin, and a very ancient one at that. The historical and cultural atmosphere into which Israelite legislation best fits — its "situation in life," to repeat again the more technical expression employed by form criticism — carries us back to before the Exile. For some laws, this is ancient Oriental jurisprudence, or more precisely, the Chanaanite code; for others, it is the origin of Yahwism in the days of Moses and Josue; for still others, the period of the sanctuary of Silo or the glorious era of the First Temple (the era of David, who prepared its foundations, and of Solomon, who completed the construction) ; and for others, finally, the period of close collaboration between the priests and the prophets as it existed when Yahwism was on the rise (Moses was a Levite and a prophet), and when friendly agreement existed between the priests and the *nebîîm* under the lofty patronage of Samuel. Besides, even in the opinion of the Wellhausen school, hardly any laws among the glosses and additions are directed against the pagan institutions or customs of post-Exilic times; almost all are concerned with the abominations of the land of Chanaan as it was before the Exile. Now, if the glosses turn out to be of an origin antedating the catastrophe of 586, *a fortiori* such is also the case with the documents into which they have been incorporated to complete, explain, or modify their primitive meaning. Moreover — and in this we have an excellent confirmatory proof — contrary to the opinion of the Wellhausen school, post-Exilic times make a very poor "situation in life" for the legislation of the

Pentateuch. Several critics agree that a perusal of the writings of the age of Esdras and Nehemias shows that sacerdotal concerns were not in the foreground. If any code can be thought to have had an influence on this age, it is Deuteronomy, or we might say a new edition of Deuteronomy.[15]

After what has just been said relative to the origins of the Hexateuch, the second major problem of literary criticism raised by the Wellhausen school may be considered as solved: the relation between the Law and the prophets. Wellhausen's position can no longer be sustained. Even critically speaking, the main body of Israelite legislation, both religious and civil, precedes the prophetical movement, which began with Elias and Eliseus in the course of the ninth century and was anticipated by Samuel and even by Moses. The classic prophets did not commit their moral teaching to an utterly blank page. At their coming the Israelite soul appeared, rather, as a palimpsest. Their work was reform and their message was a call for a return to tradition. No doubt the past was never fully revived. All reforms, even when they simply propose the restoration of past morality, are so carried away by their own impetus that they exceed this limit. That, unquestionably, is what happened in the prophetic reform. The fact, however, does not militate against the sincerity of the prophets in invoking the authority of the

---

15. Prophetic and Messianic tendencies are admittedly manifest in Deuteronomy. See, for example, Volz's study of Messianism. Canon Van Hoonacker was very well aware of the special nature of this code. See Coppens, *Le chanoine Albin Van Hoonacker*, 26-8, 56-7, 65-7, 74. — The progress achieved in the study of Deuteronomy can be noted by perusing the work of A. R. Hulst, *Het Karakter van den Cultus in Deuteronomium* (Wageningen, 1938). See the present writer's *Chronique d'Ancien Testament*, 14-15.

ancient Mosaic and nomadic traditions. They had no need
of tricks of propaganda.

As reformers of the present from a desire of preserv-
ing the past, the prophets proved to be collaborators of the
levitical priesthood. Opposition between the priesthood
and the prophets, such as that described by the Wellhausen
school, never existed. There may well have been differences and disagreements between the two institutions, and
perhaps even occasional conflicts in which the prophets
represented the progressive wing of Yahwism. But the
opposition was never radical. The present author prefers
to picture their mutual relations as they are depicted by
Welch, the Scotch exegete to whom more than once reference has already been made.[16]

The Wellhausen school considered prophetism not
only from the standpoint of the Law but also in relation
to the origins of national and Messianic eschatology. The
critics were influenced by Wellhausen's theory to postpone
to the Exile and even later the first clear manifestations of
Messianic hopes and eschatological dreams. The Gunkel-
Gressmann school has convincingly refuted them on these
two articles of the Israelite Credo.[17] We must not forget,

---

16. Welch, *Prophet and Priest in Old Israel*. Read also Kaufmann,
"Probleme der israelitisch-jüdischen Religionsgeschichte," *ZAW*, VII
(1930), 23-43, X (1933), 35-47.

17. The distance covered can be estimated by comparing the conclusions of Gunkel, Gressmann, and Mowinckel with those of Volz as
set forth in a youthful production dedicated to Julius Grill, *Die vorexilische Jahweprophetie und der Messias* (Göttingen, 1897).

For the already old Protestant views on Messianism, see: C. H.
Graf, *L'idée messianique dans son développement historique* (Strassburg,
1836); M. Hartmann, *Les prophéties messianiques et leurs principaux
interprètes modernes* (Strassburg, 1857); M. Vernes, *Le peuple d'Israël
et ses espérances relatives à son avenir depuis les origines jusqu'à l'époque
persane* (*Ve siècle avant J. C.*) (Strassburg, 1871) and *Histoire des idées
messianiques depuis Alexandre jusqu'à l'empereur Hadrien* (Paris, 1874).

On recent Catholic and Protestant opinion, see: Paul de Broglie
(the famous apologist, murdered in 1895), *Les prophéties messianiques*

however, that the hopes of Israel assumed various material expressions as time went on. It would be sinning grievously against history to seek to reduce them to a few utterly simple themes, borrowed from the categories of Christian theology. Here more than elsewhere, the question is one of delicate interpretation. The colors withstand the passage of the years but the shades vary.[18]

The fourth question to be examined is that of the provenience of the Psalms. It must be admitted that reactionary criticism approaches the traditional view far less here than it did in the discussion of the Mosaic origin of the Pentateuch. There continues to exist between the tradition of Davidic origin and the theories of reformed criticism a gap that is not easily closed. It is true, however, that another trench equally as wide has been dug between reformed criticism and the Wellhausen positions, for critics now are willing to admit a large pre-Exilic royal and liturgical Psalter. Some writers, indeed, go so far as to say that the ideas, beliefs, and practices revealed

---

(2nd ed., Paris, 1904); Lagrange, *Le messianisme chez les Juifs — 150 av. J. C. à 200 ap. J. C.* (Paris, 1909); Tobac-Coppens, *Les Prophètes d'Israël;* Lagrange, *Le Judaïsme avant Jésus Christ* (Paris, 1931); R. Arconada, "La escatologia mesianica en los Salmos ante dos objeciones recientes," *Bi,* XVII (1936), 202-229, 294-326, 461-478.

The classics of conservative or prudent progressive Protestant exegesis are well known: Briggs, *Messianic Prophecy — The Prediction of the Fulfilment of Redemption through the Messiah: A Critical Study of the Messianic Passages of the Old Testament in the Order of their Development* (Edinburgh, 1886); Franz Delitzsch, *Messianische Weissagung in geschichtlicher Folge* (Leipzig, 1890); Oesterley, *The Doctrine of the Last Things* and *The Evolution of the Messianic Idea* (London, 1908); R. H. Charles, *A Critical History of the Doctrine of a Future Life in Israel, in Judaism, and in Christianity* (London, 1913); E. König, *Die messianischen Weissagungen des Alten Testaments;* Staerk, *Soter: Die biblische Erlösererwartung — I. Der biblische Christus* (Gütersloh, 1933). The last-named work considers also the much more original studies of Mowinckel and Gressmann.

18. Tobac-Coppens, *op. cit.*

in the Psalms indicate a stage of Israelite thought for which, at least in the sources of its inspiration, the reign of David is not perhaps sufficiently remote.[19]

Is there need for returning at this late point to the Wellhausen school's version of the religious history of Israel? No one intends to deny that the ideas and facts to which Wellhausen drew attention — the reform attitude of the prophets, the work of Josias, the catastrophe of the Exile, the restoration of Judaism under Esdras and Nehemias — represent influences or stages in the religious development of the Chosen People; but it is no longer possible to interpret them as the main episodes, or *a fortiori,* the turning points of this development.[20]

It will undoubtedly be asked whether the canon of reformed, or what we may call nonconformist, criticism just treated has not also by this time its future behind it,

---

19. Pedersen, *Israel: Its Life and Culture* (Oxford, 1926); *Israel,* I (Copenhagen, 1920; 2nd ed., 1934), II (Copenhagen, 1934). See the synopsis of the work and the criticisms made of it in Hölscher, "Johannes Pedersen 'Israel,'" *Theol. Stud. Krit.,* CVIII (1937-1938), 234-262. See also Pedersen, "Passahfest und Passahlegende," *ZAW,* XI (1934), 161-175.

20. See note 39 of chapter II. Professor Irwin intimates that the present writer exaggerated the significance of the anti-Wellhausen reactions. He holds that Wellhausenism has maintained its ground but, like every scientific theory, has evolved. The writer allows himself the liberty of disagreeing with his Chicago colleague. Although exception may perhaps be taken to one or other of his judgments, he believes that he is not deceiving himself in speaking generally of a real anti-Wellhausen reaction. If it is preferred to speak of evolution, let it be admitted, at least, that it was not homogenous, that it advanced by way of mutation. To keep to a single literary problem, that of the Hexateuch: how can it be denied that the very foundations of classical Wellhausenism are threatened by doubts cast on its various theories? Discredit has come upon the Wellhausen theory on the existence of the Second Elohist, on its absolute and relative chronology for Deuteronomy, and on its estimate of the Chronicles — Eissfeldt, for one, is perfectly awake to the situation. Furthermore, what is to be said of the reaction in the fields of archæological history and of the religious history of Israel?

and whether it is more easily reconciled with the demands of Christian faith than was the canon of classical Wellhausenism.

Since the charismatic gift of prophecy is not the author's, it is difficult to answer these questions, particularly the first one. However, a brief reply may be ventured.

First, the canon of reformed criticism seems to give more promise of viability than the old Wellhausen system did. It has profited by several counter-tests, but, like every other scientific theory, it is unquestionably subject to revision. To borrow from the Duke in *Rigoletto:*

"Historical critics will vary and vary.
'Tis folly to trust them: be wary, be wary!"

But is the new criticism orthodox? To answer the question in the affirmative, one must be willing to interpret liberally the information given in the Bible on the authenticity of the inspired writings. The author believes that, in general, this can be done without prejudice to the doctrine of inspiration, since the Church has already given us a striking precedent in the case of the so-called Books of Solomon. The literary canon of nonconformist criticism, if freed from false religious and historical presuppositions, does not clash with the certainties of faith. But ecclesiastical directives must also be considered. From this angle serious reservations must be made, as we shall see later on in treating of Biblical teaching and research in Catholic universities.

However this last question is to be answered, historians of Israel must, in view of the grave inadequacies of the Wellhausen system, completely abandon the critical setting heretofore accepted, and seek for their projects a systematic approach which will be in the main new. In working up their materials and in choosing this approach, why should they not take as models the writers who in our day have revived the secular historiography of ancient and modern times? Years ago, Ewald did not shrink from putting himself in the school of Niebuhr; today likewise, closer association between the sacred and profane branches of learning can produce excellent results.

II. Historical Criticism of the Old Testament and Biblical Teaching in Seminaries

In the presence of the enormous amount of critical work of which but a faint outline has been traced in these pages, Catholic exegesis obviously cannot remain indifferent or fold its arms with a feeling of complacent superiority, treating the critical theories as so many fantastic hypotheses or as a rationalistic plague, and imagining that this is enough for victory. Abusive language cannot pass for currency in the marts of science. Can we imagine, moreover, that the stupendous work accomplished by scholars many of whom, despite our first impressions, were never animated by any hostility to Judeo-Christian traditions, has produced nothing but straw houses which the least puff of supposed good sense suffices to overturn? Certain theses, we must not forget, still enjoy the unanimous support of the critics; that concerning the Deutero-Isaias is one of them. Not only would it be very strange, but it would mean that we should have to despair of historical method if not of human reason itself, should all of this work prove to be worthless. In other spheres Catholic historians employ precisely these methods as a marvelous instrument of scientific research. Why should principles which apply to the study of documents of the patristic, mediæval, and modern ages suddenly lose their worth in the case of the inspired writings? Who would dare assert that they do? Who in practice could act as if they did?

Catholic exegetes must, therefore, reckon with historical criticism: "Vivere non est necesse, navigare necesse est!" However — and this is a qualification to be insisted on — they need not do so to the same degree and with the same precision for all grades of instruction. In teaching Scripture in our seminaries especially, critical questions should take second place. A word of explanation is in order.

First of all, historical criticism, whatever its intrinsic importance, is only an auxiliary science of exegesis. It is the vestibule from which the corridors leading to the various departments of Biblical learning branch out. Called in to guide our steps in the preliminaries of exegesis, it should withdraw as soon as this purpose is accomplished. When the mind is orientated correctly, the student should read the Sacred Text itself and its explanation should be begun. Some textbooks certainly delay too long on the enumeration of authorities and the explanation of opinions for and against the authenticity of the books, the while they forget the one thing necessary — study of the inspired writings themselves. One leaves the perusal of such works with a heavy spirit, with no love of Holy Scripture, and without any positive knowledge of the inspired doctrine.

One has not gone beyond the doormat of orientation. One has remained, so to speak, in the cloak-room.[21]

Secondly, historical criticism generally presupposes a knowledge of linguistics which the average run of seminarians does not possess and cannot be asked to acquire. In the study of the Old Testament, ignorance of Hebrew presents a serious difficulty. Neither a few odds and ends of Hebrew vocabulary, nor the explanation of a few Hebraisms will help a seminarian to understand, for example, the internal arguments for or against the authenticity of an inspired book.

Moreover, even apart from the knowledge of linguistics which it ordinarily presupposes, literary criticism is at one and the same time a science and an art, very difficult to handle. A widespread opinion holds, it is true, that whereas philosophy is the special domain of a chosen few, history is within the grasp of everyone. Unfortunately, such is not the case. Perhaps everyone is capable of getting together a good bibliography, of jotting down notes, or even of publishing a huge shelf-filler of erudition; but rare are those who succeed in digesting historical fare, and in elevating their exposition to a level whereon it is trans-

---

21. A teacher should avoid treating special and technical questions in the lecture hall, but he cannot disregard them in his personal studies. Every teacher knows by experience that only a deep and, if possible, exhaustive knowledge of the questions he has to teach enables him to give a simple, clear, and substantial exposition of them. It is the mediocre scholar who confuses issues. Fortunate are the seminary teachers who have never finished studying and who do not yield to the temptation, so frequent in our day, of spending their time and talents on all sorts of irrelevant external activity! They have enough to do in their own field. If the head no longer reflects, what will the other members do?

The author has already noted elsewhere the advantage that lies in assigning the course on the Old Testament in seminaries to a special professor. Where only one man teaches the whole of Sacred Scripture, his attention naturally enough centers on the writings of the New Testament. See Coppens, *Pour mieux comprendre et mieux enseigner l'Histoire Sainte de l'Ancien Testament* (Paris, 1935), 73-4.

muted into broad vision of the men and events described.
It is no less difficult to grasp a subtle argument in historical criticism than to grasp a proof in philosophy or
speculative theology. Historical criticism should, accordingly, be reserved for the better students, for those who
have the time necessary for a thorough training. Dr.
Goebbels, propaganda minister of the Reich, exaggerates
of course when he asserts that scarcely ten percent of mankind are capable of understanding an argument, and that
consequently propaganda and teaching — that perfected
and refined form of propaganda — should be carried on
by way of positive, categorical statements which motivate
the hearer and admit of no contradiction.[22] Still, it would
be poor judgment which would insist on building the edu-
cational structure even of the majority of seminarians on
strictly critical foundations.

We should never lose sight of the objective of clerical
formation. That objective is not specialization — to "know
more and more about less and less" — but rather to supply
aspirants to the priesthood with a solid synthesis of ecclesiastical learning, and with the means of communicating it
convincingly and spiritedly to the faithful whom they will
be called upon some day to evangelize and instruct. Priests

---

22. This explains the important rôle assigned to oratory in the
Nazi system of education. In Herr Hitler's opinion, eloquence is at the
root of all direct influence over the masses. He has even observed, in
Mein Kampf, that the masses are more receptive to the spoken word in
the evening than in the morning. One of the leading spirits in the German
Sudeten party, Herr Krebs, has written a book on the art of speaking:
Redner, lerne reden! However, though it is well and good to learn by
practical observation — "Fas est ab aliis doceri" — the teacher cannot
exemplify oratory with every sentence he utters: in fact, in teaching,
properly so called, oratory often tends to impair penetration of thought.
"Der Professor hört auf wo der Redner beginnt" — "The teacher ceases
to be at the very point where the speaker begins."

do not have to dispute with the faithful about the documents J E P D, but they should be able to impart the spiritual teaching which the inspired writings contain — Sacred Books which God in His goodness has bestowed upon the Church, to be, in the words of the "Following of Christ," the spiritual food of her children.[23]

Other branches based on Holy Scripture also merit the attention of the seminarian and his professor. A few of them may be mentioned.

Biblical theology, first of all, deserves very special consideration. One who rereads the excellent directives of the Apostolic Letter, *Quoniam in re biblica,* of March 25, 1906, will find that it gives Biblical theology a place of honor. Especially must the monotheistic and Messianic teachings of the Old Testament be restored to their rightful position.[24] Catholic professors formerly had at their disposal some sound works on the subject but, when criticism turned everything upside down, a goodly number of exegetes lost courage, and judging that it was now too

---

23. The need of a more theological and spiritual interpretation of the Holy Scriptures has developed in the Protestant Churches. However, certain authors of too reactionary a type are running into a dangerous fideism. Cf. F. Feldge, "Die Frage des alttest. Christuszeugnisses," *Th Bl,* XV (1936), 25-30; von Rad, "Sensus Scripturae Sacrae duplex?" *ibid.,* 30-34; H. Strathman, "Zum Ringen um das christliche Verständnis des Alten Testaments," *ibid.,* 257-260; H. Hellbardt, "Die Auslegung des Alten Testaments als theologische Disziplin," *ibid.,* XVI (1937), 129-143; Eichrodt, "Zur Frage der theologischen Exegese des Alten Testaments," *ibid.,* XVII (1938), 73-87.

In the Catholic field similar tendencies are appearing, but they are of a more reserved nature and keep within reasonable limits. They recently led to the publication of a large Biblical anthology. The present author's first reading of it left a favorable impression. The work is entitled, *Laienbibel zur Einführung ins Bibellesen mit Geleitwort des Herrn Kardinal-Erzbischofs Karl Joseph Schulte von Köln. Ausgabe A* (Freiburg in Breisgau, Herder, 1938).

24. *Enchiridion Biblicum* (Rome, 1927), 60.

difficult a task to elaborate a theology of the Old
Testament, resigned themselves to speaking of it no
longer. What a serious neglect! — and all the more in-
excusable because in this sphere we can devote ourselves
to scientific research to our heart's content. Nothing
stands in the way of our investigations. The exposition
of religious ideas and their nuances can be undertaken
without reference to literary and political history, on a
plane which transcends time and space and so avoids the
pitfalls of historical criticism. Such a doctrinal picture
would be an admirable background for a comparative
explanation of the Old Testament with the religious
teaching of the New.[25] Father Vosté and Father Ceuppens
must therefore be warmly congratulated for having
through their publications revived Biblical theology.[26]

---

25. See an attempt at such comparative explanation by C. G.
Montefiore, one of the most brilliant representatives of liberal Judaism,
The Old Testament and After (London, 1923) ; C. G. Montefiore and
H. Loewe, *A Rabbinic Anthology* (London, 1938).

26. J. M. Vosté: *Studia Paulina* (Rome, 1928) ; *Studia Ioannea*
(2nd ed., Rome, 1930) ; *Studia Theologiae Biblicae N. T.* (3 vols., Rome,
1933, 1934, 1937) ; F. Ceuppens; *De prophetiis messianicis in Antiquo
Testamento* (Rome, 1935) ; *Theologia Biblica* (in course of publica-
tion): *I. De Deo Uno* (Rome, 1938), *II. De Sanctissima Trinitate*
(Rome, 1938), *III. De Incarnatione et Redemptione — Pars Prima, De
Incarnatione* (Rome, 1939). See the recent outstanding work of P.
Heinisch, *Theologie des Alten Testaments,* Die Heilige Schrift des Alten
Testaments ser. (Bonn, 1940) ; also other publications cited in Coppens,
Pour mieux comprendre ... L'Histoire Sainte, 80-81, and the numerous
articles published through the initiative of Canon Pirot in the supplement
to *Le Dictionnaire de la Bible.*

Among the numerous Protestant and Reformed manuals of Old
Testament theology may be mentioned: A. C. Knudson, *The Religious
Teaching of the Old Testament* (New York, 1918) ; E. König, *Theologie
des Alten Testaments;* Maynard, *The Birth of Judaism: A Study of
Hebrew Religion during the Exile* (London, 1928) ; Sellin, *Theologie
des Alten Testaments: Israelitisch-jüdische Religionsgeschichte* (Leipzig,
1933) ; L. Köhler, *Theologie des Alten Testaments* (Tübingen, 1936) ;
Eichrodt, *Theologie des Alten Testaments: I. Gott und Volk* (Leipzig,
1933), *II. Gott und Welt* (Leipzig, 1935), *III. Gott und Mensch*
(Leipzig, 1939).

A solid course in the history of Israel is, secondly, a desideratum for all seminarians; it is indispensable for the student of Bible history and of Christian apologetics. The important literary observations which our students will need could be inserted here when treating of sources.[27] There should, however, be no long delays on critical difficulties. In view of the wide divergence of opinion on points such as the composition of the Pentateuch, the literary provenience of the Psalms, and the paternity of the book of the Consolation of Israel (Is. xl-lvi), it is wise to disregard them. This is to follow the advice of some good exegetes whose orthodoxy is

---

27. See the essay of E. Magnin, "L'Ancien Testament. Préparation évangélique," *Apologétique,* 243-315, and the rules given in Coppens, *op. cit.,* 53-56. Attention might also be called to a fine Dutch-Protestant popularization of Bible history in 22 volumes: D. J. Baarslag, *Oud-Israël* (Baarn, Bosch en Keuning, 1939). And perhaps it is opportune to mention the new complete course in Bible history being worked out under the present author's direction by the Sisters of Vorselaar (province of Antwerp, Belgium). Four booklets have already been published, of which *Gewijde Geschiedenis van het Oude Testament: Leidraad bij het Onderricht voor den 3en en 4en Graad van de Lagere School* (Averbode, 1939), is especially recommended. Another new booklet on the religious history of the Old Testament was scheduled to be published in 1940, first in Flemish and later in French.

For seminarians the author has already proposed the following courses of lectures, to occupy two hours a week over a period of four years:

General Introduction (one hour)

1. On the inspiration and canon
2. Text, versions, and exegetes
3. Outline of the political and cultural history of Israel
4. Outline of the religious history of Israel

Lectures on Exegesis (one hour)

1. Selected texts from the prophetical books
2. The great Messianic texts
3. Selected texts from the sapiential books
4. An approach to the Psalter through selected texts.

above suspicion;[28] we may mention the editors of the
Bible des Jeunes specifically. The Psalter and the Book
of the Consolation of Israel should be taken up when
the epoch in which these writings exercised the greatest
influence is being treated. The origin and content of
the Pentateuch should be treated in connection with the
era of Moses, and again with the era of Nehemias and
Esdras because of the renewal of influence which it then
enjoyed and which led to Pharisaism and Rabbinism. A
more detailed explanation of this plan and its application
can be sought in the little work already cited, *Pour mieux
comprendre et mieux enseigner l'Histoire Sainte de
l'Ancien Testament.* Perhaps the plan there proposed
could be supplemented advantageously by a chapter on
the royal literature of Israel up to the times of David
and Solomon. That would afford an opportunity to re-
place in its historical and traditional context the literature
of the psalmists and sages of Israel.

Lastly, attention should be drawn to a third important
aspect of exegesis, its æsthetic or literary side. There
was a time when it was fashionable to approach the

---

28. Coppens, *Pour mieux comprendre . . . l'Histoire Sainte,* 34-5,
71-2. — Obviously young students must not be allowed to get the impression that the correct view of the history of Israel is being kept from
them or that the truth is being partly suppressed. The professor is perfectly candid when he addresses his pupils somewhat as follows: "I cannot leave you ignorant of the fact that critical problems are raised in
regard to our Biblical documents. It is impossible to enter into the
details of these disputes, especially since the science of criticism itself
has so far been unable to settle all the difficulties. For the time being
it is enough that you know that, whatever the outcome, these disputes
cannot throw doubt on any article of faith. The Church declares the
solutions offered to be inconclusive, and she continues in the main to
hold the traditional position. Since the Scriptures influenced centuries of
human activity, we may legitimately employ them for different eras in
our reconstruction of the history of Israel. Thus, among other advan-
tages, we are enabled to avoid critical pitfalls and to build on ground
where the danger of eventual collapse is as limited as possible."

Sacred Books from the literary standpoint. An effort was made to instil a taste for reading them by enumerating and extolling all their beauties. The success of critical theories contributed largely to the neglect of this fascinating aspect of the sacred writings. The practice came to be sneered at as literary dilettantism. And yet, literary and æsthetic appreciation of the Scriptures is useful as well for true philological comprehension of these ancient documents as for the religious and homiletical formation of clerics. The sacred writers show remarkable powers of expression. The best preaching has in every age benefitted by drawing on them, for their force is timeless. An interpretation of the Scriptures which will devote more attention to the æsthetic is consequently desirable, and the future professor of exegesis would do wrong if he did not cultivate his poetic sensibilities.[29] In a lecture entitled *L'art d'approcher les chefs-d'oeuvre littéraires* and delivered before the humanists assembled at Strassburg on April 20, 1938, for the third Guillaume Budé Congress, Abel Bonnard very ably brought out this need of an æsthetic explanation of old texts. "In days gone by," said the eminent Academician, "our teachers were not wells of learning, but they knew the essentials. They could form taste and arouse admiration for masterpieces, sometimes even in the slowest member of the class, who was not necessarily the dullest. They were truly literary men, even though erudition was not their forte. The

---

29. See, for example, A. Wünsche, *Die Schönheit der Bibel: I. Die Schönheit des Alten Testaments* (Leipzig, 1903); B. Wielenga, *De Bijbel als Boek van Schoonheid* (5th ed., Kampen, 1939). Catholics would be fortunate in having a work of their own similar to Jane T. Stoddart's *The Old Testament in Life and Literature* (3rd ed., London, n. d.; 1st ed., 1913) and *The New Testament in Life and Literature* (London, n. d.).

scholar is an ant and the literary man is a bee. A point of erudition, certainly, is not always without its use, but [the savants who fancy erudition for its own sake] are like astronomers who would deliberately sprinkle dust on the lens they train on a star." This is the simple truth, admirably put. It should be taken into account in teaching, even in seminaries.

There is reason for inviting seminary professors to give preference in their teaching to synthesis rather than to analysis, to historical interpretation rather than to erudition. Priests stand in great need of a few good, all-embracing viewpoints. If we are no longer able to give to the young people whom it is our duty to educate a vital synthesis of world history, and especially of Judeo-Christian origins, they will look elsewhere for it; and some myth of the twentieth, or some other century, will come along to stock their minds. The need of synthesis, the "quest for unity," is inherent in the human mind, from that of the primitives down to that of present-day people. Historical criticism is powerless to change it.[30]

III. Old Testament Criticism, University Instruction, and Scientific Research

Although elementary, intermediate, and even higher instruction in seminaries can to a great extent usefully abstain from considering critical problems, the case of university instruction and research is quite different.

---

30. On the teaching of the sacred sciences in seminaries, see in future *Sacra Congregatio de Seminariis et Studiorum Universitatibus: Enchiridion Clericorum — Documenta Ecclesiæ alumnis instituendis* (Rome, 1938).

Scientific history can never venture a reconstruction of the physiognomy of the past until a strictly objective and critical inventory of the sources has been drawn up and placed at its disposal.

Faced with this necessity, the Church has not many policies among which to choose. Only two present themselves. Either she must isolate herself and abstain from historical investigation altogether, or she must cultivate this science according to the most rigorous canons of methodology.

It is not to be supposed that the authorities responsible for the management of ecclesiastical affairs have ever seriously entertained the first alternative. Of course the Church should not count too much on science as an instrument of the apostolate. People are not converted by a barrage of syllogisms and philological subtleties. However, science can render service to faith as a defensive weapon. It shelters the faithful against enemy attack, overcomes their hesitancies, and anticipates their difficulties. Through it the faithful are able to integrate their beliefs with the great systems of human learning, to which no man with any claim to cultural endowment can remain a stranger. Because the rôle of science is so subordinate, in exceptional circumstances the Church could, strictly speaking, decline its aid and present herself to the world shorn of all scientific trappings, with nothing but the magnificence of her faith, the heroism of her virtues, and the marvel of her miracles. Nor does this hypothetical situation belong entirely to the realm of imagination. It has been realized more than once in history, when the Church, harassed, persecuted, hampered in her activity, and impoverished, has retired into the catacombs, with no other weapons to polish than the evangelical counsels of her Master.

In more normal times, however, the Church is a generous mother and a zealous protector of humanism in the widest sense of the word. She insists on promoting all disciplines which enrich the intellectual heritage of mankind, historical science included. She is anxious, moreover, to prove to the world that there is no conflict between the order of grace and the order of nature.

Even within her ranks, therefore, the Church is careful to foster Old Testament criticism. Those to whom she appeals to fulfil this mission should answer the invitation by a wholehearted consecration of themselves and all their powers to the difficult task. Complete abstention, it must be stressed, the attitude of evangelical renouncement of the goods of this world including those of science, would be far better than imperfect mastery of the scientific disciplines which (let us never forget it) non-believers have, whether we like it or not, the right to observe if not to control. They, and perhaps also some Catholics of weak faith, would look for and find in our sophisms and in our ill-constructed hypotheses and conclusions, the excuse they are waiting for in order to reject and dismiss Christian dogma.

It is somewhat embarrasing to recall these truisms here. All Catholic scholars fully subscribe to them. The reminder, however, may not be useless, when we consider that some independent or Protestant writers persist in believing and asserting that the employment of objective history is rendered impossible in the Church and that

Christian exegesis finds itself in blind alleys.[31] They appeal especially to two lines of argumentation, well-known now to everybody. They claim first, that the Church tries *a priori* to bind scientific exegesis down to the patristic tradition; and, secondly, they point to the ecclesiastical directives of a "para-scientific" nature promulgated by the Biblical Commission since the outbreak of the Modernist crisis.[32] These objections are manifestly serious and deserve closer examination.

The difficulties which arise from the authority of the Church and of the Fathers over the Holy Scriptures are normally the result of misunderstanding. The Protestant or independent thinker whom we have in mind does not know, or does not sufficiently consider, the Catholic doctrine in the matter. The authority of the Fathers is rigorously circumscribed by the principles of fundamental theology. It is invoked only in cases, less numerous than our opponents imagine, where there is question of the Deposit of Faith and where the Fathers speak unanimously as witnesses of the Faith, proposing

---

31. Protestant and independent authors who violently, and at times bitterly, accuse the Catholic Church of a narrow conservatism in the matter of Holy Scripture might be reminded that there is no dearth of narrow conservatism in their own camp. Perhaps the best-known representative of this tendency is the clergyman, W. Möller (*Die Einheit und Echtheit der fünf Bücher Moses*, Bad Salzuflen, 1931; *Einleitung in das Alte Testament*, Zwickau, 1934). Much more violent and puerile reactions against historical criticism have sprung up in the various Protestant Churches than in the Catholic Church. If some of our own exegetes have allowed themselves to be carried too far in their opposition to the progress of scientific research, the reason is often that they have fallen under the influence of Protestant conservative reaction. By way of illustration, see the attitude of the Dutch Reformed theologians as set forth in Berkouwer, *Het Probleem der Schriftkritiek* (reviewed in the present writer's *Chronique d'Ancien Testament*, 5-6).

32. See, for example, the criticism heaped upon Catholic exegesis by W. A. Irwin (*JR*, XVIII, 1938, 441-448), after the publication of *Le chanoine Albin Van Hoonacker*. See also the author's answer in *ETL*, XVI (1939), 225-228.

an interpretation in the name of the Church and formally on the plane of divine faith. If, by way of exception, the authority of one or several of the Fathers is sufficient, it must be clearly proved that they were directly commissioned by the Church, or that they manifestly represent the mind of the Church in matters of divine faith. As for the Magisterium, the supreme ecclesiastical teaching authority, when it claims its right and authority to give a definitive interpretation of the sense of the Holy Scriptures, here too, according to the terms of the Vatican Council, it does so on the plane of faith and in the provinces of morals and Christian dogma.[33]

We might go even further. If we remember what theologians teach on the differences existing between the method of faith and theology and that of purely human science, such as exegesis in its historical and philological aspects, then it becomes evident that the authoritative interpretation of Scripture in the name of the Church is in no wise opposed to the progress of Biblical science. The case of historico-philological exegesis is fairly analogous to that of Christian philosophy. We recall the courage with which Leo XIII and Cardinal Mercier vindicated the autonomy of the purely philosophical method. In so doing they succeeded in winning for Christian philosophy a place in the sun and in securing it a hearing among non-Catholics. Does that mean that the philos-

---

33. On the authority of the Church, read Matthew J. Scheeben, *Handbuch der katholischen Dogmatik*, I (Freiburg in Breisgau, 1873), 126-137. Cf. *Conc. Vat., De fide catholica*, c. 2: "Nos, idem decretum renovantes, hanc illius mentem esse declaramus ut in rebus fidei et morum, ad ædificationem doctrinæ christianæ pertinentibus, is pro vero sensu Sacræ Scripturæ habendus sit, quem tenuit ac tenet Sancta Mater Ecclesia."

opher or the exegete disregards articles of faith, i. e., in the present consideration, patristic exegesis and the teaching of the Magisterium? By no means. Like a lighthouse beacon, to use the classic comparison, these indicate the shoals to be avoided and the way to the haven of safety. But they also leave intact the philosophical, historical, and philological methods proper to the sciences subjected to their authority. Under no pretext do they interfere with their application. The light of faith does not hamper the exegete in his research. On the contrary, the more it gives him the absolute assurance that there can be no real conflict between revealed truth and reasoned truth, the more confidence can he have in his work. If it should happen that in a particular instance he does not reach the exegesis demanded by faith, he would not be taken aback. Either he would conclude that he had erred and that his work must be done over again, or else he would have to admit that the apparatus of historico-philological investigation is of itself insufficient to reach the original and fundamental meaning of all old texts. Even this latter decision would not disturb him much. How, indeed, can we claim to disclose, even with the assistance of the best instruments, the complete sense of texts whose origin, in nine cases out of ten, is lost in the deep shadows of the past?

Objections arising from ecclesiastical directives are infinitely more troublesome to solve, for the good reason that several of these decisions enter the sphere of science itself. They add to the body of their text, not references to the Councils or the Fathers, but arguments from reason, borrowed from books on the problems they propose to settle:[34] a procedure which was somewhat of an innovation at the time the decisions were given.

In answering these objections, then, it is important not to confuse issues. An effort will be made to examine all aspects of the question and to reach an objective solution and one consonant with the wishes of the Church.

For the sake of completeness, let us recall in the first place the precise nature of the unusual position in which every apologist finds himself. It is his duty to try to meet non-believers on their own ground. In endeavoring to establish the credibility of the Catholic religion as well as that of its providential precursor, the religious dispensation of the Old Testament, his starting point should be the facts accepted by all parties. It goes without saying that the apologist can scarcely hope to find the generally admitted facts except by beginning with a critical canon which his opponents will accept. Besides, argument *ad hominem,* which supposes starting from the opponent's position, will often be advantageous, not to say strictly necessary, if he does not wish to beat the air — a thing St. Paul always refused to do: "non aerem verberans."

For these reasons and for others too, the apologist can adopt provisionally and by way of argument *ad hominem* the widely accepted canon of conservative criticism. As a matter of fact there are circumstances in which he ought to do so. From these premises — a common meeting ground with our opponents and an excellent

---

34. On the Biblical Commission, read L. Pirot, "Commission biblique," *Le Dictionnaire de la Bible — Supplément,* II (1930), 103-111. The texts of the responses from Rome are assembled in *Enchiridion Biblicum — Documenta ecclesiastica Sacram Scripturam spectantia auctoritate pontificiæ commissionis de re biblica* (Rome, 1927).

stepping-stone — he can then try to prove the miraculous and supernatural character of Old Testament revelation. It is the author's personal opinion, based partly on his own experience, that such a demonstration is possible, and that, consequently, a great work in this field can be accomplished without difficulty by Catholic writers.

There can be no objection to an exegete's using, in special circumstances, critical positions as working hypotheses. In such cases, there is no question of adopting the opinion. It is rather a matter of controlling one or the other related theory, or of thoroughly examining the facts to discover to what extent the opinion is justified. The Church cannot but commend such preliminary research work, for it certainly tends to increase objective understanding of Biblical data. Now, a fact, even a Biblical fact, is always more worthy of respect than the finest theory, traditional or critical. "Let us collect facts," remarked Buffon, "that they may give us ideas."

The true place for ecclesiastical directives is unquestionably the sphere of exegesis strictly so called. There they find their full application. The investigator owes them the external submission that right order demands. Within the limits defined by fundamental theology, he likewise owes them an intellectual assent. Before employing these directives in his work, however, it is important that he try to understand them thoroughly, being careful neither to evade their implications, nor to exaggerate their scope, nor to turn them into a rigid and standardized canon of interpretation. Before we can answer the objections made against us, therefore, we must read attentively the responses of the Biblical Commission on the Pentateuch, the Book of Isaias, and the Psalter, analyze all the terms, and try to grasp the nuances. Undoubtedly, the objectors will then agrée that these responses are broader than they were accustomed to imagine.[35]

The Commission avoids accepting any hypothesis whatsoever about the Pentateuch (June 27, 1906). If it mentions the famous theory of secretaries, at which certain exegetes scoff loudly, it does so not in order to recommend it, but simply to give a concrete example of the type of hypothesis to which Catholic exegesis can have recourse. The Commission's first response, it is true, declares for the Mosaic authorship of the Pentateuch, but this pronouncement is cautiously worded. The authorship is not affirmed in a formal and positive way; rather, the right (*jus*) of critics to affirm (*affirmandi*) and uphold tenaciously as a thesis the post-Mosaic origin of these books in their entirety, is denied. The Commission's opinion on Mosaic authorship is expressed, parenthetically, in the statement of Doubt IV, and this time the formula, "salva substantialiter Mosaica authentia et integritate Pentateuchi," is particularly happy and susceptible of a broad interpretation. The present writer does not assert that the authors of the decree personally inclined toward such an explanation, nor does he in fact think that they did. The truth will be known later, perhaps, when the archives of the Commission are opened to us. It is important, however, to call attention to the term *substantialiter.* Understood in its Scholastic sense, familiar certainly to the theologian exegetes of the Commission,[36] the word opens up wide perspectives which it would be imprudent

---

35. See Coppens, *Pour mieux comprendre . . . l'Histoire Sainte,* 70-71; *"L'Ancien Testament,"* Apologétique, 1094-7.

36. Among the signatories of the decree figures the present writer's lamented fellow-countryman, Dom Laurence Janssens, O. S. B.

to neglect. No one can predict how far science will go in matters where the Deposit of Faith is not concerned.[37]

The prudence of the Commission is still more evident in its responses on the Psalter (May 1, 1910). Even for the Psalms held to be Davidic, the Commission admits the possibility of reëditings and revisions which might have altered, to some degree at any rate, their primitive character. Davidic authorship is summed up in the statement that David is the *præcipuus auctor,* the principal author, the most notable, the most eminent; from the standpoint of quantity, this literary paternity of David is indicated only by the simple denial that the Davidic Psalms are *pauca.* Expressed positively this implies that they are many. The reservations once again are formal. The Biblical Commission was conscious of the uncertainty that hovers over this problem of the provenience of the Psalter.

We come at last to a consideration of the response on the Deutero-Isaias (June 29, 1908), since the other responses can scarcely offer any difficulty to scientific exegesis. The members of the Biblical Commission have in this case especially given proof of great circumspection. No one would think of claiming that the answer to Doubt III decides the question of authenticity of Isaias xl-lxvi. The Commission itself does not claim it, since

---

37. For purely bibliographical reasons there is listed here the work of A. D. White, *History of the Warfare of Science with Theology in Christendom* (New York, 1897), 2 vols. This book was a great success and did much harm. It contains many stupidities, to say nothing of calumnies. A prudent theologian, however, can derive some amount of profit from reading it. A certain number of the historical facts it records suggest that theologians set definite lines of demarcation between the provinces of faith and science, and should warn them against jeopardizing the credibility of the Christian religion by a capricious assent to questionable opinions.

it resumes the problem in Questions IV and V. In Doubt III, the Commission simply considers the dispute from the standpoint of certain premises which it rightly declares false. In Doubts IV and V, on the other hand, it resolutely places itself on critical ground. But it is satisfied with asserting — and why should we overlook it who have no need to be more Catholic than the Pope? — that the arguments of the critics are not compelling (*cogat*), that they do not prove conclusively (*evincendum*). Such an answer does not at all imply, if one is logical, that the brief for a Deutero-Isaias is untenable. On the contrary, it implies that the thesis does not lack a certain degree of probability. Is it not characteristic, in the case of a probable opinion, not to compel adherence, not to prove apodictically, not to lead to a firm assent, but to affirm *cum formidine oppositi?* It would certainly be an exaggeration to deduce from the terms employed that the Commission itself formally states the probability of the critical thesis. Yet even a strict interpretation seems to leave to individuals the liberty of holding and expressing it, if not of teaching it. On the other hand the Biblical Commission does object to the popularization of the critical opinion by the teaching in Catholic schools. At least it should not be proclaimed a certain and definitely accepted opinion. Still, the Commission has allowed the doubt to subsist, and it has anticipated more or less the middle course commended above, that is, that seminary teaching should avoid the discussion of critical difficulties. In fact the prudent and flexible responses of the Commission do not parallel in any way the assertions of some Catholic writers who had previously expressed themselves in favor of authenticity. The author has in

mind at the moment Father Knabenbauer, in many respects an exegete of distinction. Where he claims that
authenticity is certain (he uses the adverb *certissime* in
the course of his proof), the Commission has limited
itself to the denial of the certitude of the contrary
opinion.[38]

This literal and philological interpretation of the
Commission's decrees, let us note in passing, is nothing
new and has been used by good authors. It clears up
certain objections that our opponents lodge against us.
These objections would be further reduced in number
if the interpretation could be extended in the direction
in which some excellent writers of recognized scientific
worth and of proven fidelity to the Church hope to ori-
entate Catholic exegesis. Anyone who has taken the
trouble to follow up and examine all the manifestations
of exegetical thought in the Church within the last twenty
years, must agree.[39]

---

38. J. Knabenbauer, *Commentarius in Isaiam Prophetam,* II (1st
ed., Paris, 1887), p. 7: *certissime;* p. 11: *satis patet.* In the review of
the French edition of the present work, R. Pautrel states that Father
Knabenbauer later changed his opinion. After his death, there was
found among his papers a communication of January, 1908, to the
Biblical Commission in which he asserts that the Deutero-Isaias cannot
be attributed to the prophet Isaias of the eighth century (*non posse
attribui*). Father Pautrel adds that H. Höpfl (*Introductionis in sacros
utriusque Testamenti libros Compendium,* II, 260, No. 1) had alluded
to Father Knabenbauer's change of mind. The present writer has not
been able to check this reference (see *Études,* CCXXXIX [1939], 412).

39. A history of critical exegesis in the Church before and after
the decrees of Rome would make an interesting project. The writer has
already collected not a few documents on the matter. For the moment
we must limit ourselves to essentials. Among the *Introductions* antedating the decrees, particularly to be consulted is that of F. Gigot,
Special Introduction to the Study of the Old Testament (New York,
1901). Many brief but exact bibliographical notes are given in J.
Göttsberger, *Einleitung in das Alte Testament* (Freiburg in Breisgau,
1928). On the Old Testament from a historical point of view, two rare
small works by Loisy should be consulted: *La Religion d'Israël* (1900,
limited ed. of 300 copies), and the scarce *Etudes bibliques* (2nd ed.,
revised and augmented, Paris, Picard, 1903) containing the famous

Space does not permit the throwing into the argument of all the evidence at hand. A certain amount of it can be found recorded in the author's reviews of Old Testament works, published in *Ephemerides Theologicæ Lovanienses*. Here brevity is necessary and only a minimum of facts can be considered — once again centering around the three leading questions of the Psalter, the Pentateuch, and the Deutero-Isaïas.

In the matter of the Psalter, indications of a prudently progressive exegesis are least in evidence. The fact is self-explanatory. The responses of the Biblical Commission are not too exacting. The directives are safely followed by Hudal and Ziegler, who affirm that the editing of the Psalter extends from David to Nehemias, that many Psalms go back to David, and that about a hundred antedate the Exile. At all events, several good Catholic *Introductions,* for example those of Göttsberger and of Hudal-Ziegler, and several commentaries, such as those of Peters and Herkenne, show the utmost caution on the subject of the exact number of Davidic Psalms.[40]

---

preface of 97 pages. This preface was suppressed by the author, and is not found in most of the copies placed on sale. For Loisy's final views, see his *Un Mythe Apologétique* (Paris, 1939). One might also read J. Guitton, *Portrait de M. Pouget, prêtre de la Mission, 1847-1933* (Lyons, 1936-1938), and the present writer's review of this biography in *Chronique d'Ancien Testament,* 8-9.

40. Lack of space necessitates curtailment of the list of authors. It must be sufficient here and in the following notes to name a few select spokesmen: Göttsberger, *op. cit.;* A. Hudal-J. Ziegler, *Kurze Einleitung in die Heiligen Bücher des Alten Testaments* (Vienna, 1936) ; H. Herkenne, *Das Buch der Psalmen übersetzt und erklärt* (Bonn, 1936). Herkenne is very prudent. He is satisfied with the remark, "We undoubtedly have in the Psalter genuine Davidic songs" (5). In his paraphrase of the Biblical Commission's decree, he adds that there are no unanswerable arguments against the majority of the Psalms considered Davidic because of their superscription. N. Peters, *Das Buch der Psalmen übersetzt und erklärt* (Paderborn, 1930), 34: "It is today definitely established that an appreciable number of the Psalms are certainly pre-Exilic. By far the major portion of the first half of the

Is it an illusion to think that in the critical study of the Pentateuch Catholic exegesis tends to evolve more rapidly? The condemnation of N. Schlögel and that of the article "Moïse et Josué," from the pen of the late J. Touzard, the brilliant exegete of the Institut Catholique in Paris, must not be passed over. On the other hand, however, mention must be made of the views of Johann Nikel, the daring monograph of W. Stoderl,[41] and several theories of fragments or "crystallization," or of successive revisions proposed by, among other exegetes, Göttsberger, Heinisch, and Father Vaccari.[42] If all the law and narra-

book (1-72) falls into this category, so much so that we can speak of an unbroken series of authentic Psalms of David occurring among them. Others contain ancient material, in part Davidic."

41. J. Touzard, "Moïse et Josué," *Revue du Clergé français,* XCIX (1919), 321-343, and *Dictionnaire apologétique de la Foi catholique,* III (1919), 695-755. See on Touzard, *ETL,* XVI (1939), 634-6. N. Schlögel, *Die Schriften des Alten Bundes,* I (Vienna, 1922); J. Nikel, *Grundriss der Einleitung in das Alte Testament* (Münster in Westphalia, 1924); W. Stoderl, *Beiträge zur Einleitung in das Alte Testament. I. Das Gesetz Israels und sein Ursprung* (Prague, 1933).

42. Göttsberger, *op. cit.;* Heinisch, *Das Buch Genesis übersetzt und erklärt* (Bonn, 1934), *Das Buch Leviticus übersetzt und erklärt* (Bonn, 1935), *Das Buch Numeri übersetzt und erklärt* (Bonn, 1936). The views of Father Vaccari of the Pontifical Biblical Institute are known to us particularly through the posthumous article of Lagrange, "L'authenticité mosaïque de la Genèse et la théorie des documents," *RB,* XLVII (1938), 169-172. If the writer really understands Father Vaccari's theory, he proposes as an explanation of the variants and doublets that there existed several conflicting copies and revisions of a Mosaic work originally uniform. He seems to postulate at least two revisions, the Yahwistic and the Elohistic. Perhaps he would not be opposed to admitting still others, for example, a Deuteronomic revision. The theory obviously (though remotely) recalls certain suggestions of Welch, Böhl, Albright, and Oesterley-Robinson. These men also admit various editings, revisions, and adaptations of the same laws and narratives, traceable to the different sanctuaries, or at least influenced by the traditions of the kingdom of Israel and that of Juda. What is interesting at the moment in Father Vaccari's theory is the prominence given to the alterations — the Mosaic core being understood more or less as Lagrange would desire (*art. cit.,* 164) — and the initiative taken by the professor of the Biblical Institute to have the problems peaceably resubmitted to careful investigation.

tive sections which Heinisch refuses to assign to Moses
are added up, the total is impressive. Let us also note
the posthumous publication of Canon Van Hoonacker's
views, as he propounded them to his pupils prior to 1906,
the date of promulgation of the decree of the Biblical
Commission. He never explicitly modified his opinions,
and they retain their value from the standpoint of the
history of exegesis. They deserve to be reread and thought
upon. Some day our exegetes may find in them a starting
point for a new critical theory. Lastly, the article of
Father Lagrange, which appeared in the *Revue Biblique*
the day after the death of this eminent exegete, should
be cited.[43]

A few facts of basic importance are to be noted
about the Deutero-Isaias. In the first place, there is silence
—and silence is sometimes the most eloquent of languages
— about the Isaian authorship of Isaias xl-lxvi, on the
part of the best exegetes, Canon Van Hoonacker, Father
Condamin, S. J., and others. These men are specialists
on the subject, and the Church has reason to be proud
of them. Then, there is the fact that since 1908, except

---

43. Coppens, *Le chanoine Albin Van Hoonacker,* 67-77; Lagrange,
art. cit., 162-183. The lamented exegete explains (164) the substantial
authorship somewhat as the author sees it: "We think the conclusion
possible that the Commission holds less for literary authenticity in the
case of Moses than for substantial authenticity. Furthermore, this authenticity as applied to additions made after his death would be an
authenticity resulting from the same spirit. In much the same way, the
Thomists consider as a doctrine of St. Thomas one which they vainly
seek to find in so many words in his actual writings but which in the
opinion of his followers is consonant with his thought." On the original
positions of Lagrange, read J. Chaîne, "L'Ancien Testament: Le Sémi-
tisme," *L'Oeuvre exégétique et historique du R. P. Lagrange* (Paris, n. d.
[1936]), 11-63. See also A. Allgeier, *Biblische Zeitgeschichte* (Freiburg
in Breisgau, 1937), 49-67, where we read (60): "The Pentateuch is
the product of the religious development of the Chosen People, based
on the written Law of Moses and extending from the time of Moses
down to the period following the Exile."

for textbooks, which naturally follow accepted theories,
not a single Catholic work, at least to the writer's knowledge, has attempted a scholarly and scientific defense of
the thesis for authenticity. In the third place, there are
not a few hints in various Catholic works, for example,
in Touzard, Lippl, Göttsberger, Allgeier, Hudal-Ziegler,
and J. Fischer, from which it apparently can be deduced
that some Catholic writers of distinction do not favor
pure and simple Isaian authorship for Isaias xl-lxvi. These
authors, however, express themselves with reserve, for it
must not be forgotten that the submission of Catholic
exegesis has been exemplary. Lastly, even in popular
works, such as *La Bible des Jeunes,* chapters xl-lxvi of
Isaias are restored to an Exile setting.[44] If it be observed
that similar trends are apparent for the Apocalypse of

---

44. Göttsberger, *Einleitung,* 292-3, no. 444; 292, note 2. Consult
also: Coppens, *Le chanoine Albin Van Hoonacker,* 83-4, and A. Condamin,
"Le Livre d'Isaïe," *Études bibliques* (Paris, 1905). (This latter work
says nothing on the critical problems, but refers for them to a promised
Introduction. While engaged in revising these notes for the English
edition, the present author learned from a prospectus of J. Gabalda & Cie.
[90 Rue Bonaparte, Paris] that Father Condamin will publish his long-
expected *Introduction* after a lapse of thirty-five years. It is awaited
with intense interest.) See likewise: Allgeier, *op. cit.,* 232; Hudal-
Ziegler, *Kurze Einleitung,* 191-4; *Bible des Jeunes,* 416; the very recent
work of J. Fischer, *Das Buch Isaias übersetzt und erklärt,* part 2 (Bonn,
1939). See the writer's *Chronique d'Ancien Testament,* 21-3, and the
prudent conclusions adopted by A. Robert-A. Tricot, *Initiation biblique:
Introduction à l'étude des Saintes Écritures* (Paris, 1939).
   L. Dürr, in his *Ursprung und Ausbau der israelitisch-jüdischen
Heilandserwartung* (Berlin, 1925), 143-5, seems to place during the
Exile the Ebed Yahweh poems at the very least. In *Wollen und Wirken
der alttestamentlichen Propheten* (Dusseldorf, 1926), 148, he apparently
denies to Isaias the famous Isaian apocalypse (xxiv-xxvii) and also
xxxiv-xxxv.
   We know that the prophet Isaias formed a school (viii, 16) and
that the intelligence of his disciples is contrasted with the obduracy
of the masses (viii, 16; xxix, 11). As in other respects the Deutero- and
Trito-Isaias present manifest affinities with the body of utterances unanimously admitted to be authentic, perhaps a middle course is open to
critics: they may be able to assign these passages, if not to Isaias himself, to a school of Isaian prophets.

Isaias (xxiv-xxvii), it may well be that since the promulgation of the decree of June 29, 1908, even apart from
Protestant or independent research, several new facts
have been established which do not seem to have strengthened the argument for the authenticity of Isaias xl-lxvi.

It is not enough, however, to note that some writers
actually tend to broaden the interpretation of the ecclesiastical directives, nor is it enough to stress the fact that
they are among the exegetes of firmly established scientific
reputation and proven fidelity to the Church. We must
still ask whether such a tendency can be justified in the
light of ecclesiastical discipline and, if it can be, whether
the Church will be disposed to approve of it.

It can be asked, theoretically, whether any serious
reasons still stand in the way of the dissemination of the
more liberal interpretation. We have already seen that
the Faith does not enter into the question,[45] and we know,
moreover, that the interpretation of non-infallible decrees
admits of development.[46] On the question of fact noth-

---

45. Let it be said once and for all that it seems difficult to try to
settle questions of authenticity by recourse to the words of the Fathers,
the inspired writers, the Apostles, and Christ Himself. When these
witnesses conform to the views of their contemporaries in attributing
the Sacred Books to their traditional authors, do they really intend to
settle a problem of criticism? Are they speaking on the plane of faith
and as witnesses to it? Is it not dangerous to involve their authority,
and more importantly, that of Christ, in the solution of our puny
philological quarrels? There are enough difficulties to solve without
adding on those which are the result of our sometimes faulty understanding of Holy Writ. Father Billot used to say in theology class
that he was not annoyed by God-revealed mysteries, but by those created
by certain false theological hypotheses.

46. There is a classic example of adapting a Pontifical decree to
the exigencies of new situations in the pronouncement on the *Comma
Ioanneum* (*Enchiridion biblicum*, 46-7; Coppens, *Pour mieux comprendre . . . l'Histoire Sainte,* 70-71). On the shifting of position by
theologians in regard to the official text of the Vulgate apropos of
Sixtus V's Bull, *Aeternus ille,* and the new work of Clement VIII, see
A. Merk, "Bibel und Bulle Sixtus' V," *Scholastik,* II (Valkenburg, 1927),

ing can be said, since it belongs to the Church alone to determine its attitude regarding them. However, exegetes are allowed, indeed it is their duty, to draw attention to newly ascertained data which may justify in the eyes of authority the direction research is taking. On this score, facts can be introduced into the discussion which will apparently help greatly in the understanding and placing in proper historical setting of a development which has taken place or is still on the way to completion.

Moreover, we are now in a better position to understand why the first interpretations of the Pontifical directives greatly restricted liberty and reduced to a minimum the concessions made or permitted to criticism, not to say positively intended for it. We must picture the anguish of the Church when the plague of Modernism was at its height. Philological and historical exegesis were literally besieged, with no time for the mustering of forces. Caught unaware, the Church had at its disposal neither seasoned troops nor a complete plan of defense. To cap the climax, confusion was rampant in the ranks of Catholic exegesis itself and the Church could not trust all her defenders. What was to be done in such a situation? The Church could only call back her soldiers and draw them up in strong retreat positions in simple formation which offered no opportunity for ambush or encircle-

---

515-540, and also M. Meinertz, *Einleitung in das Neue Testament* (4th ed., Paderborn, 1933), 66-7.

These facts are not of a nature to make us uneasy. They would disturb us only if we were to forget that the ecclesiastical directives were not promulgated *ne varietur*. Based on scientific considerations as they are, they are not necessarily expected to demand rigid application forever and ever and to leave no margin for development in interpretation. The branch of science to which they apply is bound to make some progress, at least over a long period such as the thirty odd years here being considered.

ment. If we are allowed to continue the comparison, we may say that the responses of the Commission represent the defense measures adopted during the Modernist crisis by the ecclesiastical high command. The plan succeeded admirably, the maneuver was masterfully executed, the rank and file of the army held out loyally.

We need not prove that the defeat of Modernism, the genial accord existing among the workers, and the moderation which minds sometimes classified as progressive are showing, have changed the situation. The new conditions consequently allow the elaboration and defense of more liberal interpretation.

It will be well now to delay a little in setting forth what circumstances seem to the author to have most favored the progress of studies. Exegesis has in the first place been freed from the distress occasioned by the state of siege which existed at the time of the Modernist trouble. It can breathe freely once again. Even those classed as conservatives are showing themselves less timid. Secondly, the collapse of the classical Wellhausen system, especially in its religious and historical phases, has also contributed to the restoration of tranquillity in the ranks. Criticism was formerly feared as an engine of war trained against the positions of the Faith. Now that Modernism has been put out of commission and independent criticism has in great measure sorted out the false, the true, and the probable, even ecclesiastical circles are no longer worried. Thirdly, with the plague checked, the Church has come to realize that the Modernist virus did not come precisely from critical problems about authenticity. Increasing evidence shows that its source was elsewhere, particularly in philosophic assumptions. This the encyclical

Pascendi has brilliantly demonstrated.[47] Lastly, specialization in sacred studies, today recognized and sanctioned in advanced ecclesiastical instruction including that of the universities of Rome, is leading theologians to place much greater confidence in exegetes.[48] Where could writers be found today who would think of settling, on the sole basis of a few principles of speculative theology, problems which arise from the historical method?

Apart from the present favorable conditions, it must also be observed that the authors of the more liberal interpretation do not, at least consciously, overstep the limits of the ecclesiastical decrees. They are sincere in believing that they start from a perfectly legitimate interpretation and that they evolve only in proportion as advance appears to have been actually realized. The substantial Mosaic origin of the content and even of the literary form of the Pentateuch is retained, but the notion of what this substance is has become less rigid and renders

---

47. It may be remarked that the latest Modernist manifesto, *Der Katholizismus: Sein Stirb und Werde,* von katholischen Theologen und Laien, herausgegeben von Gustav Mensching (Leipzig, 1937), refrains from forging its weapons out of the conclusions of Old Testament literary criticism. The section entitled *Die moderne Bibelkritik* is taken up entirely with a few problems of the New Testament. Obviously the Modernist threat comes from other quarters.

Mensching's work adds nothing new to Modernist thought except perhaps a certain degree of moderation in expression. It has already been put on the Index, and the present writer does not think it is likely to exercise any particular show of ability. Both skins and wine are old. Rahner's article in *Zeitschrift für katholische Theologie,* LXII (1938), 109-123. Authors not courageous enough to strip off anonymity are reviving theses heard before, but they have not succeeded in presenting them with any particular show of ability. Both skins and wine are old.

48. Pii PP XI, "Constitutio Apostolica 'Deus Scientiarum Dominus' de Universitatibus et Facultatibus Studiorum ecclesiasticorum (die 24 maii 1931)," *Acta Apostolicæ Sedis,* XXIII (1931), 241-262; S. C. de Seminariis et Studiorum Universitatibus, "Ordinationes ad constitutionem apostolicam 'Deus scientiarum Dominus' de Universitatibus et Facultatibus Studiorum ecclesiasticorum rite exsequendum (die 12 iunii 1931)," *ibid.,* 263-284.

more possible a scientific investigation of the problem. Likewise, the pre-Exilic origin of a great number of the Psalms is firmly held, and there is no hesitancy in admitting a Davidic foundation for them, provided the number of which this foundation is said to be demonstrated with certitude by the critical method alone is not too greatly multiplied. Lastly, unanimity of critical opinion on the problem of the Deutero-Isaias and the persistence of this opinion throughout the anti-Wellhausen reactions previously sketched, seem to win for it, at the very least, added weight of extrinsic probability. It is thought that the affirmation of the Deutero-Isaian origin of the Book of the Consolation of Israel is, to assert nothing more, a probable opinion. And this is merely formulating what the Biblical Commission virtually had left to be inferred.

The progress just described has been made without contracting the least taint of historical and religious Wellhausenism — those two phases of the critical theory whose weakness these pages have demonstrated. It is, furthermore, vigorously opposed to those literary conclusions of the Wellhausen school whose frail, not to say entirely erroneous, character is luminously apparent after the various reactions of what has here been called nonconformist criticism.

The definitive positions of Catholic criticism probably will not be attained soon. There are minds which serve as motors and minds which serve as brakes. Provided their interaction is not accompanied by friction, and all parties meet in an atmosphere of good will and peaceful collaboration, it is advantageous to have representatives of the two types in the same school. From the clash of ideas comes light, and from the mutual control of assertions the golden middle course is opened up as time goes on.[49]

Hence we are in a position to reply to the difficulties proposed by independent exegetes. It cannot be denied that the Church has placed restrictions on scientific exegetical research. Nevertheless this strict regulation has worked out to the advantage of scholars. It put them on their guard against the fascinations of a system whose weaknesses the investigations of Protestant and independent savants have since disclosed. Catholic workers were accordingly spared the heavy penance which so-called liberal exegesis has had to perform in burning what it once adored, and in returning to positions which it should never have abandoned. While time is decanting the too rich wine of criticism, the Church is adapting her positions to meet what many consider the no longer debatable results of progressive scholarship. If the development thus nursed along can continue prudently and without that rash enthusiasm which vitiates all causes, even good ones, Catholic exegesis will soon have drawn profit from the positive results of historical criticism, the results which have withstood the wear and tear of time and the process of checking and rechecking. Thereafter nothing will prevent it from feeling absolutely at ease in scientific circles.

We can, it therefore appears, give an adequate answer to those who persist in throwing up to us as objectionable the ecclesiastical directives on scientific exege-

---

49. There is a priceless indication of this fortunate development and of the revival of exegesis in Catholic circles in Robert-Tricot, *Initiation biblique*. This work appeared under the patronage and with the collaboration of Cardinal Tisserant, president of the Pontifical Biblical Commission.

sis.[50] They have no right to picture these decrees as so
many petrified texts, destined to collectivize and stan-
dardize exegetical research once and for all. The pro-
nouncements made no pretense to infallibility and their
prime purpose was to regulate instruction. Promulgated
in strict dependence on the scientific movement, they cannot and must not pretend to be independent of it. On
the contrary, living interpretation, of course under the
control of the Church, must be applied to clear up and
adapt their meaning. In the period of crisis, as we have
seen, such interpretation was restricted; it can be allowed
more freedom now that we live in a time of peace and
harmonious development.

At the conclusion of these considerations, it is in
order to point to the provinces of textual criticism,
archæology, and Oriental linguistics. In these fields
Catholic exegesis did not cease, even in the most trying
days, to produce scientific work, and it can list names
which are recognized in all circles. Attention should also
be called to the generous encouragement which Pius XI,
of glorious memory, gave to those devoting their energies
to the cause of exegesis. The occasion was an allocution
to the select and scholarly group convened to assist at
the defense of the theses of Giorgio Castellino. The
dominant idea of the Pontiff's address was that a great

---

50. Such is the case of W. A. Irwin (*JR*, XIX, 382-386). The
present author's answer to him (see *supra*, note 39 of chapter II) does
not seem to have convinced him. It is to be hoped that a closer study
of the explanation will relieve him of the nightmare that the Church is
ghetto-izing or Hitlerizing the human intellect. If the author may use
his own work as an example, it certainly is a practical refutation of the
charge. Far from confining his readers to a ghetto, he has been able
to open the doors and windows wide so that they may have a broad
outlook on scientific work no matter in what quarter it is being
accomplished.

deal remains to be accomplished in all provinces of Biblical science. And Pius XI repeated twice: "Nil actum si quid agendum."[51]

GENERAL CONCLUSIONS

In the course of the study now drawing to an end, it was necessary to read many books, to endeavor to synopsize their substance, and to state it in a few general theses. Despite good will, there has been the constant risk of sacrificing detail to synthesis, nuance to prime color, and personages in the limelight to the backdrop of the scene. Much reflection has likewise been required in order to draw from this immense literature some directives which colleagues in the field anxious to have a part in the struggle might turn to profit.

There are in this matter of exegesis, as in so many others, two policies easy to adopt — that of criticizing *a priori* the data of tradition and the decrees of authority, and that of winding the horn and proclaiming from the housetops that all is well in the best of worlds. Both of them are seriously prejudicial to Catholic truth. Exegetes, of course, have comparatively little to say in

---

51. "Il Santo Padre . . . stava anzi per dire ad essi di dilatare le loro ambizioni come fa anche il Papa e proprio in gran parte sotto lo stimolo che il Dio delle scienze Gli dà attraverso di loro. . . . Specialmente in tema di studi biblici vi è bisogno di una direzione tassativa intorno alla critica del Sacro Testo. . . . E' invece proprio il caso di dire *Nil actum si quid agendum,* nulla è fatto finchè resta qualcosa da fare. Nella sola direzione della critica, non lo studio di una traduzione o dell'altra o degli usi anche liturgici, ma proprio per la critica del Sacro Testo, della parola divina bisogna veramente dicere: *nil actum,* poiche veramente resta tanto da fare. Era dire questo e il Papa voleva dirlo in primo luogo a Se stesso quanto resta ancora da fare per l'adempimento del proprio dovere e dire altresi a quei figlioli la legittima aspettativa che il Sommo Pontefice ha della loro cooperazione nella direzione degli alti studi specie biblici fino all'esatta comprensione delle cose." Osservatore Romano, No. 118, May 21, 1938.

the Church, but they should assert that little courageously. They should realize that their calling is not so much a trade or profession as a duty and an apostolate in which no one can take their place. Knowledge is not infused, as a rule, even in the Church. It is the fruit of patience, of persistent and humble toil. And it is well that this is the case, for it imparts to learning a reserve and modesty which are its best credentials in the eyes of the public and the authorities alike.

As regards this volume, the author has done his best (to quote a French journalist): "de ne parler ni d'un trépied comme un oracle ni d'une chaire comme un détenteur de la verité, ni d'un Sinaï comme un prophète." A desire to be of service has been the animating spirit behind this setting forth of the results of research. They are only too probably not free from inaccuracy; but there is always the hope of perfecting them in the future. For there is something satisfying in the words of St. Bernard, "Finis libri sed non finis quaerendi." Once again the daily task is accomplished, but the work, God willing, is not yet finished.

INDEX OF NAMES